SAME·DAY RESUME

write an effective resume in an hour

Second Edition

MICHAEL FARR

Also in JIST's Help in a Hurry Series

- *Same-Day Resume*
- *15-Minute Cover Letter*
- *Next-Day Job Interview*
- *Next-Day Salary Negotiation*
- *Seven-Step Job Search*
- *Overnight Career Choice*
- *90-Minute College Major Matcher*
- *Today's Hot Job Targets*

jist Works
America's Career Publisher

PART OF JIST'S HELP IN A HURRY™ SERIES

SAME-DAY RESUME, SECOND EDITION

© 2007 by not JIST Publishing

Published by JIST Works, an imprint of JIST Publishing, Inc.
8902 Otis Avenue
Indianapolis, IN 46216-1033
Phone: 1-800-648-JIST   Fax: 1-800-JIST-FAX   E-mail: info@jist.com

Visit our Web site at **www.jist.com** for information on JIST, free job search tips, book chapters, and ordering instructions for our many products! For free information on 14,000 job titles, visit **www.careeroink.com**.

Quantity discounts are available for JIST books. Have future editions of JIST books automatically delivered to you on publication through our convenient standing order program. Please call our Sales Department at 1-800-648-5478 for a free catalog and more information.

Trade Product Manager: Lori Cates Hand
Technical Contributor: Kirsten Dixson, Brandego
Interior Designer: Aleata Howard
Page Layout: Toi Davis
Cover Designer: Katy Bodenmiller
Proofreader: Paula Lowell
Indexer: Tina Trettin

Printed in the United States of America
11 10 09 08 07 06   9 8 7 6 5 4 3 2 1

    Library of Congress Cataloging-in-Publication Data
Farr, Michael.
    Same-day resume : write an effective resume in an hour / Michael Farr. -- 2nd ed.
      p. cm.
    Includes index.
    ISBN-13: 978-1-59357-383-6 (alk. paper)
    ISBN-10: 1-59357-383-9 (alk. paper)
   1. Résumés (Employment)--Handbooks, manuals, etc. 2. Job hunting. I. Title.
    HF5383.F322 2007
    650.14'2--dc22
                        2006028738

ISBN-13: 978-1-59357-383-6

ISBN-10: 1-59357-383-9

About This Book

Writing a resume doesn't have to be difficult. You can do a simple one in about an hour, and a few more hours will give you a very nice resume. That's what chapters 1, 2 and 3 are about: getting an acceptable resume finished quickly. My point is to help you get your resume done today, so that you can get started on your job search this afternoon. After all, your desire is not to do a perfect resume—it is to get a perfect job.

But this book consists of a lot more than resume advice. After you've done your resume, you can learn about cover letters, thank-you notes, and the innovative JIST Card—a mini-resume for getting the word out quickly about your skills and qualifications—in chapter 4.

Chapter 5 shows you how to adapt your resume for use on the Internet, including some tips on the latest innovations in blogs and Web portfolios. Chapter 6 shows you how to go back, when you have time, and refine the resume you created in earlier chapters.

And finally, chapter 7 is a stupendous collection of more than 50 real resumes written and designed by professional resume writers from the Career Masters Institute. You can use these samples to get ideas for the wording, layout, and design of your own resume.

In short, this little book gives you all the information you need to get your resume into employers' hands today—so that you can start getting interviews that will lead to job offers. Good luck!

Contents

A Brief Introduction to Using This Book

M ost people spend too much time worrying about their resumes. Instead, this book shows you how to write an acceptable resume in just an hour or so, and then a better one later, if you need one.

Because you obviously want to put together a resume, I assume that you are also looking for a job or are thinking about doing so. That being the case, here are my suggestions on the best way to use this book:

1. **Read the Table of Contents.** This introduces you to the content of the book and its chapters.

2. **Complete a basic resume as described in chapters 1, 2, and 3.** These short chapters *show* you how to put together a resume that will be fine for most situations—and help you do this in just a few hours. You might also want to review the sample resumes in chapter 7 to help you do your own resume.

3. **Create and circulate your JIST Card, as described in chapter 4.** A JIST Card is a mini-resume that will get your foot in the door in places where a resume might not.

4. **Begin looking for a job.** Once you have a basic resume and JIST Card, see the sidebar on pages 12–13 for a quick review of self-directed job search techniques. These techniques can reduce the time it takes to find a job. You can also read chapter 5 on Internet resumes and job search tips, in case you plan to use the Internet. Then go out looking for your next job.

5. **If you really need to, and as time permits, write a better resume.** Although it will take more time, you might want to revise your resume and create one that is, well, better. Chapter 6 provides lots of good information and sample resumes to help you in this task. But keep in mind that your priority is to get a good job and *not* to stay home working on your resume.

Of Course, You Can't Just Read About It...

To get results, you will have to actively apply what you learn in this book. One of the biggest reasons some people stay unemployed longer than others do is that they sit at home waiting for someone to knock on their door, call them up, or make them an offer via e-mail. That passive approach too often results in their waiting and waiting, while others are out there getting the offers.

I know you will resist completing the worksheets. But, trust me—they are worth your time. Doing them will give you a better sense of what you've accomplished, what you are good at, what you want to do, and how to go about doing it.

The interesting thing is that, when you finish this book and its activities, you will have spent more time planning your career than most people do. And you will know more than the average job seeker about writing a resume and finding a job.

Why This Is a Short Book

I've taught job seeking skills for many years, and I've written longer and more detailed books than this one. Yet I have often been asked to tell someone, in a few minutes or hours, the most important things they should do in their career planning or job search. Instructors and counselors also ask the same question because they have only a short time to spend with the folks they're trying to help.

I've thought about what is most important to know, if time is short. This book is short enough that you can scan it in a morning and write a basic resume that afternoon. Doing all the activities and making the improvements suggested in chapter 6 take more time but prepare you far better.

I've written this book to help you over the resume hurdle. It will help you get a resume done quickly and go about the more important task of getting a job. I hope it helps.

Chapter 1

Quick Tips for Creating and Using a Resume

This book's objective is to help you get a good job in less time. Creating a superior resume alone will not get you a job. No matter how good your resume is, you will still have to get interviews and do well in them before you get a job offer.

So, a legitimate question might be "Why have a resume at all?" This chapter answers that question by presenting both sides of the argument as well as my own conclusions. I also give you an overview of some guidelines for writing your resume and tips on how to use it.

What Is a Resume?

As a first step in creating a resume, examine what a resume is and consider what it can and cannot do.

The word "resume" describes a one- or two-page summary of your life and employment history. Although resumes traditionally have been submitted on paper, they are now frequently sent in electronic form over the Internet. Whatever a resume's form, the idea is to select specific parts of your past that demonstrate that you can do a particular job well.

A resume presents you to prospective employers who—based on their response to the resume—may or may not grant you an interview. Along with the application form, the resume is the tool employers use most often to screen job seekers.

So, a resume is clearly a tool to use in getting a job, right? The answer to this is both yes and no. Unfortunately, many people who write resume books give very bad job search advice. They confuse the purpose of a resume and, I think, put entirely too much emphasis on using it as a way to get interviews and jobs.

Some People Say You Don't Need a Resume

For a variety of reasons, many career professionals suggest that resumes aren't needed at all. Some of these reasons make a lot of sense and are detailed in the following sections.

Resumes Aren't Good Job Search Tools

It's true; resumes don't do a good job of getting you an interview. Trying to get an interview by submitting lots of unsolicited resumes is usually a waste of effort. When used in the traditional way, your resume is more likely to get you screened out than screened in. There are better ways to get in to see people, such as networking with people you know and just picking up the phone to talk to those you don't.

Five Easy Ways to Develop a Network of Contacts
1. Make lists of people you know.
2. Contact them in a systematic way.
3. Present yourself well.
4. Asks contacts for leads.
5. Contact these referrals and ask them for leads.

Some Jobs Don't Require Resumes

Employers of office, managerial, professional, and technical workers often want the details that a resume provides. But for many jobs, particularly entry-level, trade, or unskilled positions, resumes typically aren't required.

Some Job Search Methods Don't Require Resumes

Many people get jobs without using a resume at all. In most cases, these people get interviews because the employer knows them or they are referred by someone. In these situations, a resume might help but is usually not required.

Some Resume Experts Call a Resume by Another Name

Many other names are used in place of the word "resume," including "professional job power report," "curriculum vitae," "employment proposal," and other terms. One resume book author, for example, advises you not to use a resume. Instead, he advises you to use his "qualifications brief." In all their forms, though, they are really various types of resumes.

Some Good Reasons Why You Should Have a Resume

In my opinion, there are several good reasons to have a resume.

Employers Often Ask for Resumes

If an employer asks for a resume (and many do), why make excuses? This alone is reason enough to have one.

Resumes Help Structure Your Communications

A good resume requires you to clarify your job objective; select related skills, education, work, or other experiences; and list accomplishments—and present all this in a concise format. Doing these things is an essential step in your job search, even if you don't use the resume.

If Used Properly, a Resume Can Be an Effective Job Search Tool

A well-done resume presents details of your experiences efficiently so that an employer can refer to them as needed. It can also be used as a tool to present the skills you have to support your job objective and to present details that are often not solicited in a preliminary interview.

Resume Basics

I've developed some basic guidelines for developing your resume. These aren't rules, but you should carefully consider the suggestions because they are based on many years of experience and, I think, they make good common sense.

Many of these guidelines assume a traditional, printed-on-paper format rather than a resume that is submitted electronically (more on that in chapter 5). But you will likely need a paper resume *and* an electronic resume, and this advice will help in either case.

TIP: *If you show your resume to any three people, you will probably get three different suggestions on how to improve it. So, one problem with resumes is that everyone is an expert, but few of these experts agree. This means that you will have to become your own expert and make some decisions on how to do your resume. I'm here to help.*

Length

Opinions differ on length, but one to two pages is usually enough. If you are a recent high school or college graduate (within the last five years), regardless of what field you are going into, you should keep your resume to one page. If you are seeking a managerial, professional, or technical position—where most people have lots of prior experience—two pages is the norm. In most cases, a busy person will not read a resume that is any longer than two or three pages. Shorter resumes are often harder to write; but when you do them properly, they can pay off.

If you can't get everything on one page, you are better off filling up two full pages with content or more white space around the resume sections than providing one-and-a-half pages of content.

Honesty Is the Best Policy

Some people lie on their resumes and claim credentials or pay history that they don't have, hoping that no one will find out. Many organizations now verify this information, sometimes long after a person is hired.

People lose their jobs over such lies. So never lie on your resume. But that does not mean that you have to present negative information! Make sure that everything you put in your resume supports your job objective in some direct way. If you really can do the job you are seeking, someone will probably hire you. You will sleep better, too.

Eliminate Errors

I am amazed how often an otherwise good resume has typographical, grammar, or punctuation errors. Employers who notice will not think kindly of you. So dont have any! (Actually, this should be "don't have any!" which, if you did not notice, should encourage you to pay attention here.)

Even if you are good at proofreading, find someone else who is good at proofreading also and ask this person to review your resume—carefully. If possible, wait at least one day after you've written it (or longer, if you can) before reading your draft. A day's delay will allow you to notice what your resume says, rather than what you think it says.

Then, after you've read your resume, read it again to make sure you catch the errors. Then go over it again.

Appearance

Obviously, your resume's overall appearance will affect an employer's opinion of you. In a matter of seconds, the employer will form a positive or negative opinion. Is your resume well laid out? Is it crisp and professional looking? Does it include good use of white space? Does it have any errors?

> **TIP:** Even if you spell-check your resume on your computer, you still won't catch all the errors. For example, spell check won't tell you that you should use "their" instead of "they're" in cases that call for a possessive pronoun. So there is no substitute for proofing your resume carefully.

Word Processing

Almost all printed resumes are produced on high-quality ink-jet or laser printers with word-processing software. If you have your own computer system, you probably know how to use it. But, if you don't have a computer and printer that can produce high-quality print, have the word processing done by someone who does. Do not be tempted to use that old typewriter you have in the closet.

Most quick-print shops, including the national chains such as Kinko's and PIP, will do the word processing and printing for a modest fee. Ask to see samples of their work and fees—and be willing to go to a few places to get the quality you want.

Photocopying and Printing

Good quality ink-jet or laser-printed copies or photocopies of resumes are widely used and accepted. If you have your own computer and high-quality printer, individually printed resumes can present a better appearance than photocopies and, of course, will allow you to target your resume to a particular job or employer.

You can also take your resume to most small print shops and have them print a few hundred copies for a reasonable price. Just make certain that the quality is very good. However you produce your resume, make sure you have plenty on hand to use as needed.

Use Good Paper

Never go with cheap paper like that typically used for photocopies. Papers come in different qualities, and you can see the difference. Papers that include cotton fibers have a richer texture and feel that is appropriate for a professional-looking resume. Most stationery and office-supply stores carry better papers, as do quick-print shops.

Although most resumes are on white paper, I prefer an off-white bone or ivory color. You can also use other light pastel colors such as light tan or gray, but I do not recommend red, pink, or green tints. I don't like those colors, and I've read that most employers don't like them, either.

> **TIP:** *Always send a potential employer a thank-you note after an interview or other face-to-face meeting. Employers are impressed by and will remember candidates who follow up in this way. Thank-you notes can be handwritten or typed.*

Once you've selected your paper, get matching envelopes. You might also find matching "Monarch" size papers and envelopes. This smaller-sized paper, when folded once, makes for an inexpensive and perfectly acceptable thank-you note.

Use Action Words and Stress Your Accomplishments

Most resumes are boring. So don't simply list what your duties were—emphasize what you got done! Make sure you mention specific skills you have to do the job, as well as any accomplishments and credentials. Even a simple resume can include some of these elements.

Don't Be Humble

Like an interview, your resume is no place to be humble. If you don't communicate what you can do, who will?

Make Every Word Count

Write a long rough draft and then edit, edit, edit. If a word or phrase does not support your job objective, consider dropping it.

> **TIP:** The list entitled "Use Action Words and Phrases" in chapter 2 will give you ideas of action words to use, as will the sample resumes throughout the book.

Write It Yourself

It is most important that your resume represent you and not someone else. Although I expect you to use ideas and even words or phrases you like from the sample resumes in this book, you must present your own skills and support them with your own accomplishments.

If you do not have good written communication skills, get help from someone who does. Just make sure your resume ends up sounding like you wrote it.

Break Some Rules

This will be *your* resume, so you can do whatever makes sense to you. Most resume rules can be broken if you have a good reason.

The Most Important Rule of All: Do a Basic Resume Today

> **TIP:** In an active job search, you network and call potential employers for interviews. You don't wait for employers to respond to your resume.

In the rest of this and the next two chapters, you will learn about the types of resumes and see a few basic examples. You'll see more examples in chapter 7. Although many additional details will follow, remember that it is often far more useful to you to have an acceptable resume as soon as possible—and use it in an active job search—than to delay your job search while working on a better resume. A better resume can come later, after you have created a presentable one that you can use right away.

Types of Resumes

Generally the most common and useful resume types are the chronological resume, the skills (or functional) resume, and the combination resume. I also mention the curriculum vitae (CV), which is used for some specialized professional careers.

Chronological Resumes

The word "chronology" refers to a sequence of events in time. The primary feature of this type of resume is the listing of jobs you've held, listed in reverse order from the most recent to least recent. This is the simplest of resumes and can be a practical format if you use it properly. Chapter 2 shows you how to create this basic type of resume.

Because a chronological resume organizes information by your work experience, it highlights previous job titles, locations, dates employed, and tasks. This is fine if you are looking for the same type of job you have held in the past or are looking to move up in a related field.

The chronological resume presents a career progression and allows employers to quickly screen out applicants whose backgrounds are not conventional or do not fit the preferred profile. The chronological format is often not good for people who have limited work experience (such as recent graduates), want to do something different, or have less-than-ideal work histories such as job gaps.

Skills, or Functional, Resumes

Rather than list your experience under each job, this resume style clusters your experiences under major skill areas. For example, if you are strong in "communication skills," you could list a variety of work and other experiences under that heading.

This format makes little sense, of course, unless your job objective *requires* these skills. For this reason and others, a skills resume is often more difficult to write than a simple chronological resume. But if you have limited paid work experience, are changing careers, or have not worked for a while, a skills resume might be a better way to present your strengths.

A skills resume is often used in situations where the writer wants to avoid displaying obvious weaknesses that would be highlighted on a chronological resume. For example, someone who has been a teacher but who now wants a career in sales could clearly benefit from a skills resume. A skills resume can help hide a variety of other weaknesses as well, such as limited work experience, gaps in job history, lack of educational credentials, and other flaws. This is one reason why some employers don't like skills resumes—they make it harder for them to quickly screen out applicants.

Personally, I like skills resumes. Assuming that you honestly present what you can do, a skills resume often gives you the best opportunity to present your strengths in their best light. Chapter 3 shows you how to write your own skills resume.

Combination and Other Creative Resumes

You can combine elements of both the chronological and skills formats in various ways to improve the clarity or presentation of a resume. This is often a good compromise when your experience is limited but an employer still wants to see a chronological listing of your work history (as many do). You can begin the resume with a skills format but still include a section that lists your jobs in order, along with the dates you held them.

There are also creative formats that defy any category but that are clever and have worked for some people. These resumes use innovative formats and styles. Some use dramatic graphics, colors, and shapes. I've seen hand-written resumes (usually *not* a good idea); unusual paper colors, sizes, and shapes; resumes with tasteful drawings and borders; and lots of other ideas. Some of these resumes were well done and well received; others were not. Graphic artists, for example, might use their resumes as examples of their work and include various graphic elements. An advertising or marketing person might use a writing style that approximates copywriting and a resume design that looks like a polished magazine ad.

The Curriculum Vitae and Other Special Formats

Attorneys, college professors, physicians, scientists, and various other occupations have their own rules or guidelines for preparing a "Professional Vitae" or some other special format. If you are looking for a job in one of these specialized areas, you should learn how to prepare a resume to those specifications. These specialized and occupation-specific resumes are not within the scope of this book and examples are not included, but many books provide information on these special formats.

"Send Your Resume to Lots of Strangers and, If It Is Good Enough, You Will Get Job Offers" and Other Fairy Tales

> **TIP:** Contrary to the advice of many people who write resume books, writing a "dynamite" or "perfect" (or whatever) resume will rarely get you the job you want. That will happen only following an interview, with just a few odd exceptions. So the task in the job search is to get interviews and to do well in them. Sending out lots of resumes to people you don't know—and most other traditional resume advice—is a lot of baloney (or, if you prefer, bologna).

As I will say throughout this book, your objective is to get a good job, not to do a great resume. I have written this book to teach you the basics of putting together a useful and effective resume, but any resume will only be as good as how you use it. And the big problem with resumes is that most people don't understand that a resume is not a good job search tool at all.

That is why I suggest doing a simple resume early in your job search—one you can create in a few hours. This "same-day" approach allows you to get on with actively getting interviews instead of sitting at home working on a better resume. Later, as you have time, you can do an improved resume.

Seven Steps to Getting a Job Fast

Here are the key elements of getting a good job in less time:

1. **Know your skills.** If you don't know what you are good at, how can you expect anyone else to figure it out? One employer survey found that about 80 percent of those who made it to the interview did not do a good job presenting the skills they had to do the job. If you don't know what you are good at and how this relates to a particular job, you can't write a good resume, can't do a good interview, and are unlikely to get a good job.

2. **Have a clear job objective.** If you don't know where you want to go, it will be most difficult to get there. You can write a resume without having a job objective, but it won't be a good one.

3. **Know where and how to look.** Because three out of four jobs are not advertised, you will have to use nontraditional job search techniques to find them.

4. **Spend at least 25 hours a week looking.** Most job seekers spend far less than this and, as a result, are unemployed longer than they need to be. So, if you want to get a better job in less time, plan on spending more time on your job search.

5. **Get two interviews a day.** It sounds impossible but this *can* be done once you redefine what counts as an interview (see the sidebar at the bottom of this page). Compare getting two interviews a day to the average job seeker's activity level of four or five interviews a month, and you can see how it can make a big difference.

6. **Do well in interviews.** You are unlikely to get a job offer unless you do well in this critical situation. I've reviewed the research on what it takes to do well in an interview and found, happily, that you can improve your interview performance relatively easily. Knowing what skills you have and being able to support them with examples is a good start. Chapter 3 helps you identify your key skills and prepare for interviews—as well as write a superior resume.

7. **Follow up on all contacts.** Following up can make a big differ-ence in the results you get in your search for a new job.

No one should ever say that looking for a job is easy. But I have learned that you can take steps to make the process a bit easier and shorter than it typically is. Getting your resume together is something that hangs up many people for entirely too long. The next two chapters should help you solve that problem.

The New Definition of an Interview

An interview is any face-to-face contact with someone who has the authority to hire or supervise a person with your skills—even if no opening exists at the time you talk to them.

Chapter 2

Do a Simple Resume in About an Hour

You *can* write a basic resume in about an hour. It will not be a fancy one, and you might want to write a better one later, but I suggest you do the simple one first. Even if you decide to create a more sophisticated resume later (see chapter 6), doing one now will allow you to use it in your job search within 24 hours.

Chronological Resume Basics

A chronological resume is easy to do. It works best for people who have had several years of experience in the same type of job they are seeking now. This is because a chronological resume clearly displays your recent work experience. If you want to change careers, have been out of the workforce recently, or do not have much paid work experience related to the job you want, a chronological resume might not be the best format for you. In these instances, you might want to use a skills resume, which is presented in chapter 3.

Most employers will find a chronological resume perfectly acceptable, as long as it is neat and has no errors. You can use it early in your job search while you work on a more sophisticated resume.

> **TIP:** The important point is to get together an acceptable resume quickly so that you won't be sitting at home worrying about your resume instead of being out job hunting.

Two Chronological Resume Samples

Two sample chronological resumes for the same person follow. The first (figure 2-1) is a simple one, but it works well enough in this situation because Judith is looking for a job in her present career field, has a good job history, and has related education and training. Note that she wants to move up in responsibility, and her resume emphasizes the skills and education that will assist her.

One nice feature is that Judith put her recent business schooling in both the Education and Experience sections. Doing this filled a job gap and allows her to present recent training as equivalent to work experience. This resume includes the extra Personal section, where she presents some special strengths that often are not included in a resume.

The second example (figure 2-2) is an improved version of this same resume. The improved resume adds a number of features, including a more thorough job objective, a Special Skills and Abilities section, and more accomplishments and skills. Notice, too, the impact of the numbers she adds to this resume in statements such as "top 30 percent of my class" and "decreased department labor costs by more than $30,000 a year."

> **TIP:** *If you will be submitting your resume to resume databases or via e-mail, this format will require only minor modification. Fancier resumes with graphics, bullets, lines, and dressy fonts must be stripped of their more decorative elements to become electronic resumes. Chapter 5 has much more detail on writing and formatting your resume for use on the Internet and with resume databases.*

You should be able to do this sort of resume with an hour or two of additional work over the preceding one. As I think you will realize, most employers like the additional positive information it provides.

Writing the Major Sections of a Chronological Resume

Now that you have seen what both basic and improved chronological resumes look like, it's time to do your own chronological resume. Use the Instant Resume Worksheet beginning on page 27 to complete each part of your basic chronological resume.

Name

This one seems obvious, but you want to avoid some things. For example, don't use a nickname—you need to present a professional image. Even if you have to modify your name a bit from the way you typically introduce yourself, it might be appropriate.

Figure 2-1: A Simple Chronological Resume

Judith J. Jones

115 South Hawthorne Avenue
Chicago, Illinois 66204
(312) 653-9217 (home)
email: jj@earthlink.net

JOB OBJECTIVE

Desire a position in the office management, accounting, or administrative assistant area. Prefer a position requiring responsibility and a variety of tasks.

EDUCATION AND TRAINING

Acme Business College, Lincoln, Illinois
Graduate of a one-year business program.

John Adams High School, South Bend, Indiana
Diploma, business education.

U.S. Army
Financial procedures, accounting functions.

Other: Continuing-education classes and workshops in business communication, computer spreadsheet and database programs, scheduling systems, and customer relations.

EXPERIENCE

2002–present—Claims Processor, Blue Spear Insurance Co., Wilmette, Illinois. Handle customer medical claims, develop management reports based on spreadsheets I created, exceed productivity goals.

2001–2002—Returned to school to upgrade my business and computer skills. Took courses in advanced accounting, spreadsheet and database programs, office management, human relations, and new office techniques.

1998–2001—E4, U.S. Army. Assigned to various stations as a specialist in finance operations. Promoted prior to honorable discharge.

1997–1998—Sandy's Boutique, Wilmette, Illinois. Responsible for counter sales, display design, cash register, and other tasks.

1995–1997—Held part-time and summer jobs throughout high school.

PERSONAL

I am reliable, hardworking, and good with people.

Figure 2-2: An Improved Chronological Resume

Judith J. Jones

115 South Hawthorne Avenue • Chicago, Illinois 66204
(312) 653-9217 (home)
e-mail: jj@earthlink.net

JOB OBJECTIVE

Seeking position requiring excellent business management skills in an office environment. Position should require a variety of tasks, including office management, word processing, and spreadsheet and database program use.

EDUCATION AND TRAINING

Acme Business College, Lincoln, Illinois.
Completed one-year program in Professional Office Management. Grades in top 30 percent of my class. Courses included word processing, accounting theory and systems, advanced spreadsheet and database programs, time management, and basic supervision.

John Adams High School, South Bend, Indiana.
Graduated with emphasis on business courses. Earned excellent grades in all business topics and won top award for word-processing speed and accuracy.

Other: Continuing-education programs at my own expense, including business communications, customer relations, computer applications, sales techniques, and others.

EXPERIENCE

2002–present—Claims Processor, Blue Spear Insurance Company, Wilmette, Illinois. Handle 50 complex medical insurance claims per day, almost 20 percent above department average. Created a spreadsheet report process that decreased department labor costs by more than $30,000 a year (one position). Received two merit raises for performance.

2001–2002—Returned to business school to gain advanced skills in accounting, office management, sales, and human resources. Computer courses included word processing and graphics design, accounting and spreadsheet software, and database and networking applications. Grades in top 30 percent of class.

1998–2001—Finance Specialist (E4), U.S. Army. Responsible for the systematic processing of more than 200 invoices per day from commercial vendors. Trained and supervised eight employees. Devised internal system allowing 15 percent increase in invoices processed with a decrease in personnel. Managed department with a budget equivalent to more than $350,000 a year. Honorable discharge.

1997–1998—Sales Associate promoted to Assistant Manager, Sandy's Boutique, Wilmette, Illinois. Made direct sales and supervised four employees. Managed daily cash balances and deposits, made purchasing and inventory decisions, and handled all management functions during owner's absence. Sales increased 26 percent and profits doubled during my tenure.

1995–1997—Held various part-time and summer jobs through high school while maintaining good grades. Earned enough to pay all personal expenses, including car and car insurance. Learned to deal with customers, meet deadlines, work hard, handle multiple priorities, and develop other skills.

SPECIAL SKILLS AND ABILITIES

Quickly learn new computer applications and am experienced with a number of business software applications. Have excellent interpersonal, written, and oral communication and math skills. Accept supervision well, am able to supervise others, and work well as a team member. Like to get things done and have an excellent attendance record.

Mailing Address

Don't abbreviate words such as "Street" or "Avenue." Do include your ZIP code. If you might move during your job search, ask a relative, friend, or neighbor whether you can temporarily use his or her address for your mail. As a last resort, arrange for a post office box. Forwarded mail will be delayed and can cause you to lose an opportunity; get an address at the new location so you appear to be settled there.

> **TIP:** Look at the many sample resumes in chapter 7 to see how others have handled things. Those resumes present lots of good ideas.

Phone Numbers and E-mail Address

An employer is more likely to phone or send an e-mail than to contact you by mail. So giving an employer this contact information is essential.

Let's start with the telephone. Use a phone number that will be answered throughout your job search. Always include your area code. Because you often will be gone (at your current job or out job seeking, right?), you must use an answering machine or voice mail. Phone companies sell voice-mail services for a monthly fee, including an option of a separate voice-mail phone number. This can pay off if you worry about how your calls might be answered at home. It takes only one messed-up message to make this service worthwhile.

I suggest that you call your answering machine or voice-mail message. Listen to what it says, and how. If yours has some cute, boring, or less-than-professional message, change it to one you would like your next employer to hear. You can go back to your standard howling-wolves message after you get your next job.

> **TIP:** Keep in mind that an employer could call at any time. Make sure that anyone who will pick up the phone knows to answer professionally and take an accurate message, including a phone number. Practice with these people if you need to. Nothing is as maddening as a garbled message with the wrong number.

As you look at this book's sample resumes, notice that some provide more than one phone number or an explanation following the number. For example, "555-299-3643 (messages)" quickly communicates that the caller is likely to have to leave a message rather than reach you in person. Adding "555-264-3720 (cell phone)" gives employers another calling option.

If you have an e-mail address, include it. Many employers will appreciate having it, and it will show that you are technologically savvy.

Now, take a moment to complete the Identification section in the Instant Resume Worksheet on page 27.

Job Objective

Although you could put together a simple resume without a job objective, it is wise to include one. Doing so will allow you to select resume content that will directly support the job you want.

Carefully write your job objective so that it does not exclude you from any jobs you would consider. For example, if you use a job title like "administrative assistant," ask yourself if doing so would exclude you from other jobs you would consider. Look at how Judith Jones presented her job objective in her basic resume (figure 2-1):

> *Desire a position in the office management, accounting, or administrative assistant area. Prefer a position requiring responsibility and a variety of tasks.*

This resume opens up more options for her than if she simply said "administrative assistant." And her improved resume's job objective says even more:

> *Seeking position requiring excellent business management skills in an office environment. Position should require a variety of tasks, including office management, word processing, and spreadsheet and database program use.*

A good job objective allows you to be considered for more responsible jobs than you have held in the past or to accept jobs with different titles that use similar skills.

I see many objectives that emphasize what the person wants but that do not provide information on what he or she can do. For example, an objective that says "Interested in a position that allows me to be creative and that offers adequate pay and advancement opportunities" is not good. Who cares? This objective, a real one that someone wrote, displays a self-centered, "gimme" approach that will turn off most employers. Yours should emphasize what you can do, your skills, and where you want to use them.

Use the following worksheet to help you construct an effective and accurate Job Objective statement for your resume.

THE JOB OBJECTIVE WORKSHEET

1. What sort of position, title, and area of specialization do you want? Write the type of job you want, just as you might explain it to someone you know.

_____

_____

_____

2. Define your bracket of responsibility. Describe the range of jobs you would accept, from the minimum up to those you think you could handle if you were given the chance.

_____

_____

_____

3. Name the key skills you have that are important in this job. Describe the two or three key skills that are particularly important for success in the job that you are seeking. Select one or more of these that you are strong in and that you enjoy using. Write it (or them) here.

_____

_____

_____

4. Name any specific areas of expertise or strong interest that you want to use in your next job. If you have substantial interest, experience, or training in a specific area and want to include it in your job objective (remembering that it might limit your options), write it here.

_____

_____

_____

5. What else is important to you? Is there anything else you want to include in your job objective? This could be a value that is particularly important to you (such as "a position that allows me to help families" or "employment in an aggressive and results-oriented organization"), a preference for the size or type of organization ("a small- to mid-size business"), or something else.

_____

_____

_____

Refer to the examples of simple but useful job objectives in the following box. Most provide some information on the type of job the candidate seeks as well as on the skills he or she offers.

Sample Job Objectives

A responsible general-office position in a busy, medium-sized organization.

A management position in the warehousing industry. Position should require supervisory, problem-solving, and organizational skills.

Computer programming or systems analysis. Prefer an accounting-oriented emphasis and a solution-oriented organization.

Medical assistant or coordinator in a physician's office, hospital, or other health services environment.

Responsible position that requires skills in public relations, writing, and reporting.

An aggressive and success-oriented professional seeking a sales position offering both challenge and growth.

Desire position in the office-management area. Position should require flexibility, good organizational skills, and an ability to handle people.

The sample resumes throughout this book include job objectives that you can review to see how others have phrased them. Browse these objectives for ideas.

Now jot down your own draft job objective and refine it until it "feels good." Then rewrite it on the Instant Resume Worksheet on page 27.

> **TIP:** *The best objectives avoid a narrow job title and keep your options open to a wide variety of possibilities within a range of appropriate jobs.*

Education and Training

Lead with your strengths. Recent graduates or those with good credentials but weak work experience should put their education and training toward the top because it represents a more important part of their experience. More experienced workers with work experience related to their job objective can put their education and training toward the end.

You can drop the Education and Training section if it doesn't support your job objective or if you don't have the credentials typically expected of those seeking similar positions. This is particularly true if you have lots of work experience in your career area. Usually, though, you should emphasize the most recent or highest level of education or training that relates to the job.

Depending on your situation, your education and training could be the most important part of your resume, so beef it up with details if you need to.

Look at the sample resumes in chapter 7 for ideas. Then, on a separate piece of paper, rough out your Education and Training section. Then edit it to its final form and write it on pages 27–30 of the Instant Resume Worksheet.

> **TIP:** *Drop or downplay details that don't support your job objective. For example, if you possess related education but not a degree, tell employers what you do have. Include details of related courses, good grades, related extracurricular activities, and accomplishments.*

Use Action Words and Phrases

Use active rather than passive words and phrases throughout your resume. Here is a short list of active words to give you some ideas:

Achieved	Established priorities	Organized
Administered	Expanded	Planned
Analyzed	Implemented	Presented
Controlled	Improved	Promoted
Coordinated	Increased productivity	Reduced expenses
Created	(or profits)	Researched
Designed	Initiated	Scheduled
Developed	Innovated	Solved
Diagnosed	Instructed	Supervised
Directed	Modified	Trained
Established policy	Negotiated	

Work and Volunteer History

This resume section provides the details of your work history, starting with the most recent job. If you have significant work history, list each job along with details of what you accomplished and special skills you used. Emphasize skills that directly relate to the job objective on your resume.

Treat volunteer or military experience the same way as other job experiences. This can be very important if this is where you got most of your work experience.

Previous Job Titles

You can modify the title you had to more accurately reflect your responsibilities. For example, if your title was sales clerk but you frequently opened and closed the store and were often left in charge, you might use the more descriptive title of night sales manager. Check with your previous supervisors if you are worried about this and ask whether they would object.

> **TIP:** Look up the descriptions of jobs you have held in the past and jobs you want now in a book titled the Occupational Outlook Handbook. This book is available in most libraries. You can also find it online at the Department of Labor's Web site: www.bls.gov/oco. These descriptions will tell you the skills needed to succeed in the new job. Emphasize these and similar skills in your resume.

If you were promoted, you can handle the promotion as a separate job if it is to your advantage. Also make sure your resume mentions that you were promoted.

Previous Employers

Provide the organization's name and list the city, state, or province in which it was located. A street address or supervisor's name is not necessary—you can provide those details on a separate sheet of references.

Employment Dates

If you have large employment gaps that are not easily explained, use full years instead of months and years to avoid emphasizing the gaps. If there was a significant period when you did not work, did you do anything that could explain it in a positive way? School? Travel? Raise a family? Self-employment? Even if you mowed lawns and painted houses for money while you were unemployed, that could count as self-employment. It's much better than saying you were unemployed.

Duties and Accomplishments

In writing about your work experience, be sure to use action words and emphasize what you accomplished. Quantify what you did and provide evidence that you did it well. Take particular care to mention skills that would directly relate to doing well in the job you want now.

If your previous jobs are not directly related to what you want to do now, emphasize skills you used in previous jobs that could be used in the new job. For example, someone who waits on tables has to deal with people and work quickly under pressure—skills that are needed in many other jobs such as accounting and managing.

Use separate sheets of paper to write rough drafts of what you will use in your resume. Edit it so that every word contributes something. When you're done, transfer your statements to pages 30–33 of the Instant Resume Worksheet.

Professional Organizations

This is an optional section where you can list job-related professional, humanitarian, or other groups with which you've been involved. These activities might be worth mentioning, particularly if you were an officer or were active in some other way. Mention accomplishments or awards. Many of the sample resumes in chapter 7 include statements about accomplishments.

Now go to page 33 of the Instant Resume Worksheet and list your job-related efforts in professional organizations and other groups.

Recognition and Awards

If you have received any formal recognition or awards that support your job objective, consider mentioning them. You might create a separate section for them; or you can put them in the Work Experience, Skills, Education, or Personal sections.

> **TIP:** *Emphasize accomplishments! Think about the things you accomplished in jobs, school, the military, and other settings. Make sure that you emphasize these things in your resume, even if it seems like bragging.*

Personal Information

Years ago, resumes included personal details such as height, weight, marital status, hobbies, leisure activities, and other trivia. Please do not do this. Current laws do not allow an employer to base hiring decisions on certain points, so providing this information can cause some employers to toss your resume. For the same reason, do not include a photo of yourself.

Although a Personal section is optional, I sometimes like to end a resume on a personal note. Some resumes provide a touch of humor or playfulness as well as selected positives from outside school and work lives. This section is also a good place to list significant community involvements, a willingness to relocate, or personal characteristics an employer might like. Keep it short.

Turn now to page 33 of the Instant Resume Worksheet and list any personal information you feel is appropriate.

References

It is not necessary to include the names of your references on a resume. You can do better things with the precious space. It's not even necessary to state "references available on request" at the bottom of your resume, because that is obvious. If an employer wants your references, he or she knows to ask you for them.

It is helpful to line up references in advance. Pick people who know your work as an employee, volunteer, or student. Make sure they will express nice things about you by asking what they would say if asked. Push for negatives and don't feel hurt if you get some. Nobody is perfect, and it gives you a chance to delete references before they do you damage.

When you know who to include, type a clean list of references on a separate sheet. Include names, addresses, phone numbers, and details of why they are on your list. You can give this to employers who want it.

> **TIP:** Some employers have policies against giving references over the phone. If this is the case with a previous employer, ask the employer to write a letter of reference for you to photocopy as needed. This is a good idea in general, so you might want to ask employers for one even if they have no rules against phone references.

The Final Draft

At this point you should have completed the Instant Resume Worksheet at the end of this chapter. Carefully review dates, addresses, phone numbers, spelling, and other details. You can now use the worksheet as a guide for preparing a better-than-average chronological resume.

Use the sample chronological resumes from this chapter as the basis for creating your resume. Additional examples of resumes appear in chapters 3 and 7. Look them over for writing and formatting ideas. The sample resumes in chapter 3 tend to be simpler and easier to write and format than some found in chapter 7 and will provide better models for creating a resume quickly.

If you have access to a computer, go ahead and put the information into the form of a resume. Most word-processing programs have resume templates or "wizards" that will help make it look good. If you do not have access to a computer, have someone else do your resume. But whether you do it yourself or have it done, carefully review it for typographical or other errors that may have slipped in. Then, when you are certain that everything is correct, have the final version prepared.

INSTANT RESUME WORKSHEET

Identification

Name_____

Home address_____

ZIP code_____

Phone number and description (if any)_____

_____

Alternate phone number and description_____

_____

E-mail address_____

Your Job Objective

_____

_____

_____

_____

_____

_____

Education and Training

Highest Level/Most Recent Education or Training

Institution name_____

City, state/province (optional)_____

Certificate or degree_____

Specific courses or programs that relate to your job objective_____

_____

_____

(continued)

(continued)

Related awards, achievements, and extracurricular activities

Anything else that might support your job objective, such as good grades

College/Post High School

Institution name

City, state/province (optional)

Certificate or degree

Specific courses or programs that relate to your job objective

Related awards, achievements, and extracurricular activities

Anything else that might support your job objective, such as good grades

High School

Institution name_____

City, state/province (optional)_____

Certificate or degree_____

Specific courses or programs that relate to your job objective_____

_____

_____

Related awards, achievements, and extracurricular activities_____

_____

_____

Anything else that might support your job objective, such as good
grades_____

_____

_____

_____

_____

**Armed Services Training
and Other Training or Certification**

Institution name_____

Specific courses or programs that relate to your job objective_____

_____

_____

Related awards, achievements, and extracurricular activities_____

_____

_____

(continued)

(continued)

Anything else that might support your job objective, such as good
grades_____

_____

_____

_____

_____

Related Workshops, Seminars, Informal Learning, or Any Other Training

_____

_____

_____

_____

_____

_____

Work Experience

Most Recent Position

Dates: from_____to_____

Organization name_____

City, state/province_____

Your job title(s)_____

Duties_____

_____

_____

Skills_____

_____

_____

Equipment or software you used_____

_____

_____

Promotions, accomplishments, and anything positive_____

_____

Next Most Recent Position

Dates: from_____to_____

Organization name_____

City, state/province_____

Your job title(s)_____

Duties_____

_____

_____

Skills_____

_____

_____

Equipment or software you used_____

_____

_____

Promotions, accomplishments, and anything positive_____

_____

_____

(continued)

(continued)

Next Most Recent Position

Dates: from _____ to _____

Organization name _____

City, state/province _____

Your job title(s) _____

Duties _____

_____

_____

Skills _____

_____

_____

Equipment or software you used _____

_____

_____

Promotions, accomplishments, and anything positive _____

_____

_____

Next Most Recent Position

Dates: from _____ to _____

Organization name _____

City, state/province _____

Your job title(s) _____

Duties _____

_____

_____

Skills

Equipment or software you used

Promotions, accomplishments, and anything positive

Any Other Work or Volunteer Experience

Professional Organizations

Personal Information

Chapter 3

Write a Skills Resume in Just a Few Hours

A lthough it takes a bit longer to do a skills resume than it does a chronological resume, you should consider writing one for a variety of reasons. This chapter will show you why you might consider a skills resume and how to write one.

Be sure to read chapter 1 and do the activities in chapter 2 (particularly the Instant Resume Worksheet on pages 27–33) before completing the skills resume described here.

The Skills Resume

This chapter shows you how to write a resume that is organized around the key skills you have that the job you want requires. Although a skills resume requires more time to write than the resumes in chapter 2, its advantages might make writing one worthwhile.

In its simplest form, a chronological resume is little more than a list of job titles and other details. Employers often look for candidates with a work history that fits the position. If they want to hire a cost accountant, they will look for someone who has done this work. If you are a recent graduate or have little experience in the career or at the level you now want, you will find that a simple chronological resume emphasizes your *lack* of related experience rather than your ability to do the job.

A skills resume avoids these problems by highlighting what you have done under specific skills headings rather than under past jobs. If you hitchhiked across the country for two years, a skills resume won't necessarily display this as an employment gap. Instead, you could say "Traveled extensively throughout the country and am familiar with most major market areas." That could be very useful experience for certain positions.

Even if you don't have anything to hide, a skills resume emphasizes your key skills and experiences more clearly. And you can always include a chronological list of jobs as one part of your skills resume, as shown in some of this book's examples. So everyone should consider a skills resume.

A Sample Skills Resume

Following is a basic skills resume (figure 3-1). The example is for a recent high school graduate whose only paid work experience has been in a hamburger place. Read it and ask yourself whether you would consider interviewing Lisa if you were an employer. For most people, the answer is yes.

> **TIP:** Because skills resumes can hide your problems, some employers do not like them. But many do. Besides, if a chronological resume highlights a weakness, a skills resume might help get you an interview instead of getting screened out. Who wins? You do.

This resume presents a good example of how a skills resume can help someone who does not have the best credentials. It allows the job seeker to present school and extracurricular activities to good effect. It is a strong format choice because it lets her highlight strengths without emphasizing her limited work experience. It doesn't say where she worked or for how long, yet it gives her a shot at many jobs.

Although the sample resume is simple, it presents Lisa in a positive way. She is looking for an entry-level job in a nontechnical area, so many employers will be more interested in her skills than in her job-specific experience. What work experience she does have is presented as a plus. And notice how she listed her gymnastics experience next to "Hardworking."

> **TIP:** You might have more work experience than shown in this sample. If so, look at the sample resumes at the end of this chapter and at those in chapter 7. There are many examples of skills resumes for people with more education and experience.

The skills format can work well for a variety of situations and might be right for you. And, again, you can combine elements of the chronological and skills resume formats to get the best of both. There are several examples of combination resumes in chapter 7.

Figure 3-1: A Basic Skills Resume

Lisa M. Rhodes
813 Lava Court • Denver, Colorado 81613
Home: (413) 643-2173 (leave message)
Cell phone: (413) 442-1659
E-mail: lrhodes@netcom.net

Position Desired
Sales-oriented position in a retail sales or distribution business.

Skills and Abilities

Communications
Good written and verbal presentation skills. Use proper grammar and have a good speaking voice.

Interpersonal
Able to get along well with coworkers and accept supervision. Received positive evaluations from previous supervisors.

Flexible
Willing to try new things and am interested in improving efficiency on assigned tasks.

Attention to Detail
Concerned with quality. My work is typically orderly and attractive. Like to see things completed correctly and on time.

Hardworking
Throughout high school, worked long hours in strenuous activities while attending school full-time. Often handled as many as 65 hours a week in school and other structured activities while maintaining above-average grades.

Customer Contacts
Routinely handled as many as 500 customer contacts a day (10,000 per month) in a busy retail outlet. Averaged a lower than .001% complaint rate and was given the "Employee of the Month" award in my second month of employment. Received two merit increases. Never absent or late.

Cash Sales
Handled over $2,000 a day ($40,000 a month) in cash sales. Balanced register and prepared daily sales summaries and deposits.

Reliable
Excellent attendance record, trusted to deliver daily cash deposits totaling more than $40,000 a month.

Education
Franklin High School. Took advanced English and other classes. Member of award-winning band. Excellent attendance record. Superior communication skills. Graduated in top 30% of class.

Other
Active gymnastics competitor for four years. This taught me discipline, teamwork, how to follow instructions, and hard work. I am ambitious, outgoing, reliable, and willing to work.

Writing Your Skills Resume

The skills resume format uses a number of sections similar to those in a chronological resume. Here I will discuss only those sections that are substantially different—the job objective and skills sections. Refer to chapter 2 for information on sections that are common to both resume types. The samples at the end of this chapter give you ideas on skills resume language, organization, and layout, as well as how to handle special problems.

Don't be afraid to use a little creativity in writing your skills resume. Remember, you are allowed to break some rules if it makes sense.

Job Objective

Although a simple chronological resume does not require a career objective, a skills resume does. Without a reasonably clear job objective, you can't select and organize the key skills you have to support that job objective. The job objective statement on a skills resume should answer the following questions:

- **What sort of position, title, or area of specialization do you seek?** After reading the information on job objectives in chapter 2, you should know how to present the type of job you are seeking. Is your objective too narrow and specific? Is it so broad or vague that it's meaningless?

- **What level of responsibility interests you?** Job objectives often indicate a level of responsibility, particularly for supervisory or management roles. If in doubt, always try to keep open the possibility of getting a job with a higher level of responsibility (and, often, salary) than your previous or current one. Write your job objective to include this possibility.

> **TIP:** Review the "Sample Job Objectives" box on page 21 in the preceding chapter and look at the sample resumes at the end of this chapter and in chapter 7. Notice that some resumes use headings such as "Position Desired," "Career Objective," or "Profile" to introduce the job objective section. Many people think that these headings sound more professional than "Job Objective." It's your decision.

- **What are your most important skills?** What are the two or three most important skills or personal characteristics needed to succeed on the job you're targeting? These are often mentioned in a job objective.

The Skills Section

This section can be called Areas of Accomplishment, Summary of Qualifications, Areas of Expertise and Ability, and so on. Whatever you choose to call it, this section is what makes a skills resume. To construct it, you must carefully consider which skills you want to emphasize.

Your task is to feature the skills that are essential to success on the job you want *and* that you have and want to use. You probably have a good idea of which skills meet both criteria.

Note that some resumes in this book emphasize skills that are not specific to a particular job. For example, "well organized" is an important skill in many jobs. In your resume, you should provide specific examples of situations or accomplishments that show you possess such skills. You can do this by including examples from previous work or other experiences.

The Key Skills List

On the next page is a list of skills that are considered key for success on most jobs. It is based on research with employers about the skills they look for in employees. So if you have to emphasize some skills over others, include these—assuming you have them, of course.

Key Skills Needed for Success in Most Jobs	
Basic Skills Considered the Minimum to Keep a Job	*Key Transferable Skills That Transfer from Job to Job and Are Most Likely Needed in Jobs with Higher Pay and Responsibility*
Basic academic skills	Instruct others
Accept supervision	Manage money and budgets
Follow instructions	Manage people
Get along well with coworkers	Meet the public

Key Skills Needed for Success in Most Jobs	
Basic Skills Considered the Minimum to Keep a Job	*Key Transferable Skills That Transfer from Job to Job and Are Most Likely Needed in Jobs with Higher Pay and Responsibility*
Meet deadlines	Work effectively as part of a team
Good attendance	Negotiating
Punctual	Organize/manage projects
Hard worker	Public speaking
Productive	Written and oral communication
Honest	Organizational effectiveness and leadership
	Self-motivation and goal setting
	Creative thinking and problem solving

In addition to the skills in the list, most jobs require skills specific to a particular job. For example, an accountant needs to know how to set up a general ledger, use accounting software, and develop income and expense reports. These job-specific skills are called *job-content skills* and can be quite important in qualifying for a job.

IDENTIFY YOUR KEY TRANSFERABLE SKILLS

Look over the preceding key skills list and write down any skills you have and that are particularly important for the job you want. Add other skills you possess that you feel must be communicated to an employer to get the job you want. Write at least three, but no more than six, of these most important skills:

1. _____

2. _____

3. _____

4. _____

5. _____

6. _____

Prove Your Key Skills with a Story

Now, write each skill you listed in the preceding box on a separate sheet. For each skill, write several detailed examples of when you used it. If possible, you should use work situations, but you can use other situations such as volunteer work, school activities, or other life experiences. Try to quantify the examples by giving numbers such as money saved, sales increased, or other measures to support those skills. Emphasize results you achieved and any accomplishments.

The following is an example of what one person wrote for a key skill. It might give you an idea of how to document your own skills.

> *Key skill: Meeting deadlines*
>
> *I volunteered to help my social organization raise money. I found out about special government funds, but the proposal deadline was only 24 hours away. So I stayed up all night and submitted it on time. We were one of only three groups whose proposals were approved, and we were awarded over $100,000 to fund a youth program for a whole year.*

Edit Your Key Skills Proofs

If you carefully consider the skills needed in the preceding story, there are quite a few. Here are some I came up with:

- Hard work
- Meeting deadlines
- Willing to help others
- Good written communication skills
- Persuasive
- Problem solver

Review each "proof sheet" and select the proofs that are particularly valuable in supporting your job objective. You should have at least two proof stories for each skill area. After you select your proofs, rewrite them using action words and short sentences. In the margins, write the skills you needed to do these things. When you're done, write statements you can use in your resume. Rewrite your proof statements and delete anything that does not reinforce the key skills you want to support.

Following is a rewrite of the example proof story. Do a similar editing job on each of your own proofs until they are clear, short, and powerful. You can then use these statements in your resume, modifying them as needed.

Key skill: Meeting deadlines

On 24-hour notice, submitted a complex proposal that successfully obtained over $100,000 in funding.

You could easily use this same proof story to support other skills I listed earlier, such as hard work. So, as you write and revise your proof stories, consider which key skills they best support. Use the proofs to support those key skills in your resume.

Tips for Editing Your Draft Resume into Final Form

Before you make a final draft of your skills resume, look over the samples at the end of this chapter for ideas on content and format. Several show interesting techniques that might be useful for your situation. For example, if you have a good work history, you can include a brief chronological listing of jobs. This jobs list could be before or after your skills section. If you have substantial work history, you could begin your skills resume with a summary of experience to provide the basis for details that follow.

When you have the content from the proof stories you need for your skills resume, write or word process your first draft. Rewrite and edit it until the resume communicates what you really want to say about yourself. Cut anything that does not support your objective. When you are done, ask someone to *very carefully* review it for typographical and other errors.

If you are having someone else prepare your resume, have the "final" copy reviewed by someone other than yourself for errors you might have overlooked. Only after you are certain that your resume contains no errors should you prepare the final version.

Remember that this is your resume, so do it in a way you think presents you best. Trust your own good judgment.

Your objective is to get a good job, not to keep working on your resume. So avoid the temptation to make a "perfect" resume and, instead, get this one done. Today. Then use it tomorrow.

TIP: *If you plan to look for jobs on the Internet, chapter 5 provides information on modifying your resume for online use.*

If the urge to improve your resume comes to you, don't resist. Just work on your next resume on weekends—chapter 6 will help you. In the meantime, use the one you finished today in your job search. If all goes well, you might never need a "better" resume.

More Sample Skills Resumes

Look over the sample resumes that follow to see how others have adapted the basic skills format to fit their situations. These examples are based on real resumes (although the names and other details are not real), and I have included comments to help you understand details that might not be apparent.

The formats and designs of the resumes are intentionally basic and can be done with any word processor. Chapter 7 includes many other skills resumes, including many with fancier graphics and designs. But remember that it is better to have a simple and error-free resume—and be out there using it—than to be at home working on a more elaborate one.

Darrel Craig's Resume

This is a resume (figure 3-2) of a career changer with substantial work experience, but in another occupation. After working for an alarm and security systems company and at a variety of other jobs, Darrel went back to school and learned computer programming. The skills format allows him to emphasize his past business experience to support his current job objective. His resume includes no chronological jobs listing and no education dates, so it is not obvious that he is a recent graduate with little formal work experience as a programmer.

Darrel does a good job of presenting previous work experience and includes numbers to support his skills and accomplishments. Even so, the relationship between his previous work and current objective could be improved. For example, collecting bad debts requires discipline, persistence, and attention to detail—the same skills required in programming. And, although he is good at sales, his resume does not relate the skills required for sales to his new job objective of programming.

Darrel's job objective could be improved. If Darrel were here to discuss it, I'd ask him if he wants to use his selling skills *and* his programming skills in a new job. If so, he could modify his job objective to include jobs such as selling technology or computer consulting services. Or, if he wants to be a programmer, I would suggest he emphasize other transferable skills that directly support his programming objective, such as his history of meeting deadlines. Still, this resume is effective in relating his past business experience to his ability to be a programmer in a business environment.

Figure 3-2: Darrel Craig's Resume

Darrel Craig

Career Objective
Challenging position in programming or related areas that would best use expertise in the business environment. Position should have opportunities for a dedicated individual with leadership abilities.

Programming Skills
Experience with business program design including payroll, inventory, database management, sales, marketing, accounting, and loan amortization reports. Knowledgeable in program design, coding, implementation, debugging, and file maintenance. Familiar with distributed PC network systems (LAN and WAN) and have working knowledge of DOS, UNIX, BASIC, FORTRAN, C, and LISP plus UML, Java, C++, and Visual Basic.

Applications and Network Software
Am a Microsoft Certified Systems Engineer and familiar with a variety of applications programs including Lotus Notes, Novell and NT network systems, database and spreadsheet programs, and accounting and other applications software.

Communication and Problem Solving
Interpersonal communication strengths, public relations capabilities, innovative problem solving, and analytical talents.

Sales
A total of eight years of experience in sales and sales management. Sold security products to distributors and burglar alarm dealers. Increased company's sales from $36,000 to more than $320,000 per month. Organized creative sales and marketing concepts. Trained sales personnel in prospecting techniques and service personnel in more efficient and consumer-friendly installation methods. Result: 90% of all new business was generated through referrals from existing customers.

(continued)

(continued)

Management

Managed security systems company for four years while increasing profits yearly. Supervised 20 personnel in all office, sales, accounting, inventory, and installation positions. Worked as assistant credit manager, responsible for over $2 million per year in sales. Handled semi-annual inventory of five branch stores totaling millions of dollars.

Accounting

Balanced all books and prepared tax-return forms for security systems company. Four years of experience in credit and collections. Collection rates were over 98% each year and was able to collect a bad debt in excess of $250,000 deemed "uncollectible."

Education

School of Computer Technology, Pittsburgh, PA
Graduate of two-year Business Application Programming/TECH EXEC Program—3.97 GPA

Robert Morris College, Pittsburgh, PA

Associate degree in Accounting, Minor in Management

2306 Cincinnati Street, Kingsford, PA 15171
(412) 437-6217
(412) 464-1273 (leave message)
E-mail: Dcraig1273@aol.com

Thomas Marrin's Resume

This resume (figure 3-3) combines elements of the chronological and skills formats. Thomas's resume breaks some "rules," but for good reasons. He has kept his job objective quite broad and does not limit it to a particular industry or job title. Because he sees himself as a business manager, it does not matter to him in what kind of business or industry he works. He prefers a larger organization, as his job objective indicates. His education is near the top because he thinks it is one of his strengths.

Thomas has worked with one employer for many years, but he presents each job there as a separate one. This allows him to provide more details about his accomplishments within each position and more clearly indicate that these were promotions to increasingly responsible jobs. His military experience, although not recent, is listed under a separate heading because he thinks it is important. Note how he presented his military experience using civilian language. This is very important because most hiring managers are unfamiliar with military jargon. (See chapter 7 for more examples of civilian resumes for former military personnel.)

This resume could have been two pages, and doing so would allow him to provide additional details about his job at Hayfield Publishing and in other areas. The extra space could also be used for more white space and a less crowded look, although the resume works fine as is.

Figure 3-3: Thomas Marrin's Resume

THOMAS P. MARRIN
80 Harrison Avenue • Baldwin L.I., New York 11563
Cell Phone: (716) 223-4705
E-mail: tmarrin@techconnect.com

POSITION DESIRED

Mid- to upper-level management position with responsibilities including problem solving, planning, organizing, and budget management.

EDUCATION

University of Notre Dame, BS in Business Administration. Course emphasis on accounting, supervision, and marketing. Upper 25% of class. Additional training: Advanced training in time management, organizational behavior, and cost control.

BUSINESS EXPERIENCE

Wills Express Transit Co., Inc., Mineola, New York
Promoted to Vice President, Corporate Equipment—2000 to Present
Controlled purchase, maintenance, and disposal of 1,100 trailers and 65 company cars with more than $8 million operating and $26 million capital expense responsibilities.
• Scheduled trailer purchases for six divisions.
• Operated 2.3% under planned maintenance budget in company's second-best profit year while operating revenues declined 2.5%.
• Originated schedule to correlate drivers' preferences with available trailers, decreasing driver turnover 20%.
• Developed systematic Purchase and Disposal Plan for company car fleet.
• Restructured company-car policy, saving 15% on per-car cost.

Promoted to Assistant Vice President, Corporate Operations—1998 to 2000
Coordinated activities of six sections of Corporate Operations with an operating budget of more than $10 million.
• Directed implementation of zero-base budgeting.
• Developed and prepared executive officer analyses detailing achievable cost-reduction measures. Resulted in cost reduction of more than $600,000 in first two years.
• Designed policy and procedure for special equipment leasing program during peak seasons. Cut capital purchases by more than $1 million.

Promoted to Manager of Communications—1996 to 1998
Directed and managed $1.4 million communication network involving 650 phones, 75 WATS lines, 3 switchboards, and 15 employees.
• Installed computerized WATS Control System. Optimized utilization of WATS lines and pinpointed personal abuse.
  Achieved 100% system payback six months earlier than projected.
• Devised procedures that allowed simultaneous 20% increase in WATS calls and a $75,000/year savings.

Hayfield Publishing Company, Hempstead, New York
Communications Administrator—1994 to 1996
Managed daily operations of a large Communications Center. Reduced costs 12% and improved services.

MILITARY EXPERIENCE

U.S. Army—2nd Infantry Division, 1992 to 1994. First Lieutenant and platoon leader stationed in Korea and Ft. Knox, Kentucky. Supervised an annual budget equivalent of nearly $9 million and equipment valued at more than $60 million. Responsible for training, scheduling, supervision, mission planning, and activities of as many as 40 staff. Received several commendations. Honorable discharge.

Peter Neely's Resume

Peter lost his factory job when the plant closed. He got a survival job as a truck driver and now wants to make truck driving his career because it pays well and he likes the work.

Notice how his resume (figure 3-4) emphasizes skills from previous jobs and other experiences that are essential for success as a truck driver. This resume uses a combination format that includes elements from both skills and chronological resumes. The skills approach allows him to emphasize specific skills that support his job objective; the chronological list of jobs allows him to display a stable work history.

The jobs he had years ago are clustered under one grouping because they are not as important as more recent experience. Also, doing so does not show that he is older. Yes, I realize employers are not supposed to discriminate based on age, but Peter figures "Why take chances?" For the same reason, Peter does not include dates for his military experience or high school graduation, nor does he separate them into categories such as Military Experience or Education. They just aren't as important in supporting his job objective as they might be for a younger person.

Unusual elements are comments about not smoking or drinking and a stable family, although these comments work. Peter figures that an employer will think that a stable, healthy, and sober truck driver is better than the alternative. Also note how Peter presented his military experience as another job, with an emphasis on the truck driving and diesel experience.

Figure 3-4: Peter Neely's Resume

Peter Neely

203 Evergreen Road
Houston, Texas 39127
Messages: (237) 649-1234   Beeper: (237) 765-9876 (anywhere in the country)

POSITION DESIRED: Short- or Long-Distance Truck Driver

Summary of Work Experience: Over 15 years of stable work history, including substantial experience with diesel engines, electrical systems, and driving all sorts of trucks and heavy equipment.

SKILLS

Driving Record/ Licenses: Have current Commercial Driving License and Chauffeur's License and am qualified and able to drive anything that rolls. No traffic citations or accidents in more than 20 years.

Vehicle Maintenance: I maintain correct maintenance schedules and avoid most breakdowns as a result. Substantial mechanical and electrical systems training and experience enable me to repair many breakdowns immediately and avoid towing.

Record Keeping: Excellent attention to detail. Familiar with recording procedures and submit required records on a timely basis.

Routing: Thorough knowledge of most major interstate routes, with good map-reading and route-planning skills. I get there on time and without incident.

Other: Not afraid of hard work, flexible, get along well with others, meet deadlines, excellent attendance, responsible.

WORK EXPERIENCE

2000–Present CAPITAL TRUCK CENTER, Houston, Texas
Pick up and deliver all types of commercial vehicles from across the United States. Am trusted with handling large sums of money and handling complex truck-purchasing transactions.

1992–2000 QUALITY PLATING CO., Houston, Texas
Promoted from production to Quality Control. Developed numerous production improvements resulting in substantial cost savings.

1987–1992 BLUE CROSS MANUFACTURING, Houston, Texas
Received several increases in salary and responsibility before leaving for a more challenging position.

Prior to 1987 Truck delivery of food products to destinations throughout the South. Also responsible for up to 12 drivers and equipment-maintenance personnel.

OTHER

Four years of experience in the U.S. Air Force, driving and operating truck-mounted diesel power plants. Responsible for monitoring and maintenance on a rigid 24-hour schedule. Stationed in Alaska, California, Wyoming, and other states. Honorable discharge.

High school graduate plus training in diesel engines and electrical systems. Excellent health, love the outdoors, stable family life, nonsmoker and nondrinker.

Andrea Atwood's Resume

This resume (figure 3-5) uses a simple format with few words and lots of white space. It looks better, I think, than more crowded resumes. I would like to see more numbers used to indicate performance or accomplishments. For example, what was the result of the more efficient record-keeping system she developed? And why did she receive the employee-of-the-month awards?

As a recent high school graduate, Andrea does not have substantial experience in her field, having had only one full-time job since graduation. This resume's skills format allows her to present her strengths better than a chronological resume would. Because she has formal training in retail sales, she could have given more details about specific courses she took or other school-related activities that would support her objective. Even so, her resume does a good job of presenting her basic skills to an employer in an attractive format.

Figure 3-5: Andrea Atwood's Resume

ANDREA ATWOOD
3231 East Harbor Road
Grand Rapids, Michigan 41103
Home: (303) 447-2111

Objective: A responsible position in retail sales or marketing.

Areas of Accomplishment:

Customer Service
- Communicate well with all age groups.
- Able to interpret customer concerns to help them find the items they want.
- Received six Employee-of-the-Month awards in 3 years.

Merchandise Display
- Developed display skills via in-house training and experience.
- Received Outstanding Trainee Award for Christmas toy display.
- Dress mannequins, arrange table displays, and organize sale merchandise.

Inventory Control
- Maintained and marked stock during department manager's 6-week illness.
- Developed more efficient record-keeping procedures.

Additional Skills	• Operate cash register and computerized accounting systems.
	• Willing to work evenings and weekends.
	• Punctual, honest, reliable, and hardworking.
Experience:	Harper's Department Store
	Grand Rapids, Michigan
	2000 to present
Education:	Central High School
	Grand Rapids, Michigan
	3.6 grade-point average (4.0 scale)
	Honor Graduate in Distributive Education
	Two years of retail sales training in Distributive Education. Also courses in Business Writing, Computerized Accounting, and Word Processing.

Linda Marsala-Winston's Resume

Linda's resume (figure 3-6) is based on one included in a book by David Swanson titled *The Resume Solution*. This resume shows the style that David prefers: lots of white space, short sentences, and brief but carefully edited narrative. Short. Like promotional copy. Like this.

This is another skills resume that breaks rules because it uses a skills format; however, the skills are really ways to organize job-related tasks. Some skills include references to specific employers. So this would be considered a combination resume.

Linda's resume is short but presents good information to support her job objective. I would like to see some numbers or other measures of results, although it is clear that Linda is good at what she does. Did you notice that this resume includes no dates? You probably wouldn't notice until you had formed a positive impression. Well, it turns out that Linda did this on purpose, to hide the fact that much of her work was as a self-employed freelancer. Linda is also a bit older. She thought these things could work against her in getting a job, so she didn't include dates.

TIP: *The design for this resume is based on a resume template from a popular word-processing program. Most programs offer several predetermined resume design options that include various typefaces and other simple but effective format and design elements. This makes resume creation much easier for novices.*

Figure 3-6: Linda Marsala-Winston's Resume

Linda Marsala-Winston

6673 East Avenue

Lakeland, California 94544

(415) 555-1519 (voice mail)

lmw@netmail.net

Objective: Copywriter or Account Executive in Advertising or Public Relations Agency

Professional Experience

Copywriter

Developed copy for direct-mail catalogs featuring collectible items, for real estate developments, and for agricultural machinery and equipment.

Writer

Wrote many articles for *Habitat* magazine. Specialized in architecture, contemporary lifestyles, and interior design.

Sales Promotion

Fullmer's Department Store, Detroit. Developed theme and copy for grand opening of new store in the San Francisco Bay area.

Fabric Designer

Award-winning textile designer and importer of African and South American textiles.

Other Writing and Promotion

News bureau chief and feature writer for college newspaper, contributor to literary magazine. Script writer for fashion shows. Won creative-writing fellowship to study in Mexico. Did public relations for International Cotton Conference. Summer graduate fellow in public information, United Nations, New York City.

Education

University of California, Berkeley

Bachelor of Arts Degree in English. Graduate study, 30 credits completed in Journalism.

California State University, Fresno

Master of Arts Degree in Guidance and Counseling.

Professional Membership

San Francisco Women in Advertising

Sara Smith's Resume

This is a two-page resume (figure 3-7) based on one in a book by Richard Lathrop titled *Who's Hiring Who.* It originally was squeezed on one page. Although Richard calls it a "Qualifications Brief," this is a pure-form example of a skills resume.

This resume is unconventional in a variety of ways. It clearly takes advantage of the skills format by avoiding all mention of a chronology of past jobs. There are no references to specific employers, to employment dates, or even to job titles.

This is a clever example of how a well-done skills resume can present a person effectively in spite of a lack of formal paid work experience—or cover other problems. Students, career changers, and others can benefit in similar ways.

Figure 3-7: Sara Smith's Resume

Sara Smith
1516 Sierra Way
Piedmont, California 97435
(416) 486-3874

OBJECTIVE

Program Development, Coordination, and Administration

...especially in a people-oriented organization where there is a need to assure broad cooperative effort through the use of sound planning and strong administrative and persuasive skills to achieve common goals.

MAJOR AREAS OF EXPERIENCE AND ABILITY

Budgeting and Management for Sound Program Development

With partner, established new association devoted to maximum personal development and self-realization for each of its members. Over a period of time, administered budget totaling more than $1,000,000. Jointly planned growth of group and related expenditures, investments, programs, and development of property holdings to realize current and long-term goals. As a result, holdings increased twenty-fold over the period, reserves invested increased 1200%, and all major goals for members have been achieved or exceeded.

Purchasing to Ensure Smooth Flow of Needed Supplies and Services

Made purchasing decisions to ensure maximum production from available funds. Determined ongoing inventory needs, selected suppliers, and maintained a strong continuing line of credit while minimizing financing costs. No significant project was ever adversely affected by lack of necessary supplies, equipment, or services on time.

Personnel Development and Motivation

Developed resources to ensure maximum progress in achieving potential for development among all members of our group. Frequently engaged in intensive personnel counseling to achieve this. Sparked new community progress to help accomplish such results. Although arrangements with my partner gave me no say in selecting new members (I took them as they came), the results produced by this effort are a source of strong and continuing satisfaction to me. (See "Some Specific Results.")

Sara Smith   Page Two

Transportation Management

Determined transportation needs of our group and, in consultation with members, assured specific transportation equipment acquisitions over a broad range of types (including seagoing). Contracted for additional transportation when necessary. Ensured maximum utilization of limited motor pool to meet frequently conflicting requirements demanding arrival of the same vehicle at widely divergent points at the same moment. Negotiated resolution of such conflicts in the best interest of all concerned. In addition, arranged four major moves of all facilities, furnishings, and equipment to new locations.

Other Functions Performed

Duties periodically require my action in the following additional functional areas: Crisis management; proposal preparation; political analysis; nutrition; recreation planning and administration; stock market operations; taxes; building and grounds maintenance; community organizations; social affairs administration (including VIP entertaining); catering; landscaping (two awards for excellence); contract negotiations; teaching, and more.

Some Specific Results

Above experience gained in 10 years devoted to family development and household management in partnership with my husband, Harvey Smith, who is equally responsible for results produced. *Primary achievements:* Daughter Sue, 12, a leading candidate for the U.S. Junior Olympics team in gymnastics. A lovely home in Piedmont (social center for area teenagers). *Secondary achievements:* Vacation home at Newport, Oregon (on the beach). President of Piedmont High School PTA two years. Organized successful citizen protest to stop incursion of Oakland commercialism on Piedmont area.

PERSONAL DATA AND OTHER FACTS

Bachelor of Arts (Business Administration), Cody College, Cody, California. Highly active in community affairs. Have learned that there is a spark of genius in almost everyone that, when nurtured, can flare into dramatic achievement.

Chapter 4

The 15-Minute Cover Letter and Other Job Search Correspondence

This chapter provides advice on writing cover letters, JIST Cards, and thank-you notes. It includes various samples of each type of correspondence.

Cover Letters

Writing a simple cover letter *is* pretty simple. Once you know how it's done, you should be able to write one in about 15 minutes or so.

It is not appropriate to send a resume to someone without explaining why. It is traditional to provide a letter along with your resume—a cover letter. Depending on the circumstances, the letter would explain your situation and ask the recipient for some specific action, consideration, or response.

Entire books discuss the art of writing cover letters. Some authors go into great detail on how to construct "powerful" cover letters. Some suggest that a cover letter can replace a resume by providing information specifically targeted to the person receiving it. Although these ideas have merit, my objective here is to give you a simple, quick review of cover letter basics that will meet most needs.

If you think about it, you will send a resume and cover letter to only two groups of people:

- People you know.
- People you don't know.

Although I realize this sounds simple, it's true. And this observation makes it easier to understand how you might structure your letters to each group. First let's review some basics regarding writing cover letters in general.

Seven Quick Tips for Writing a Superior Cover Letter

No matter who you are writing to, virtually every good cover letter should follow these guidelines.

> **TIP:** *Although many situations require a formal letter, a simple note will do in many instances (for example, when you know the person you are writing to).*

Write to Someone in Particular

Never send a cover letter "To whom it may concern" or use some other impersonal opening. We all get enough junk mail. If you don't send your letter to someone by name, it will be treated like junk mail.

Make Absolutely No Errors

One way to offend people quickly is to misspell their names or use incorrect titles. If you have any question, call to verify the correct spelling of the name and other details before you send the letter. Also, review your letters carefully to be sure that they contain no typographi cal, grammatical, or other errors.

Personalize Your Content

If you can't personalize your letter in some way, don't send it. I've never been impressed by form letters, and you should not use them. Those computer-generated letters that automatically insert a name never fool anyone, and I find cover letters done in this way offensive. Although some resume and cover letter books recommend that you send out lots of these "broadcast letters" to people you don't know, I suggest that doing so wastes time and money.

Present a Good Appearance

Your contacts with prospective employers should always be professional, so buy good quality stationery and matching envelopes. Use papers and envelopes that match or complement your resume paper. Cover letters are typically printed on standard-size paper; however, you can also use the smaller Monarch-size paper with matching envelopes. For colors, I prefer white, ivory, or light beige.

Use a standard letter format that complements your resume type and format. Most word-processing software provides templates or "wizards" to automate your letter's format and design. I used such templates to create the formats for the sample letters in this chapter. And don't forget the envelope! Address it carefully, without abbreviations or errors.

Provide a Friendly Opening

Begin your letter with a reminder of any prior contacts and the reason for your correspondence now. The examples later in this section will give you some ideas on how to handle this.

> **TIP:** Cover letters are rarely handwritten anymore, and employers expect them to be word processed or typed (without error!), with excellent print quality.

Target Your Skills and Experiences

To do this well, you must know something about the organization or person with whom you are dealing. Present any relevant background that might be of particular interest to the person you are writing.

Close with an Action Statement

Don't close your letter without clearly identifying what you will do next. I do not recommend that you leave it up to the employer to contact you because that doesn't guarantee a response. Close on a positive note and let the employer know you will make further contact.

Writing Cover Letters to People You Know

It is always best if you know the person you are writing. Written correspondence is less effective than personal contact, so the ideal circumstance is to send a resume and cover letter after having spoken with the person directly.

For example, it is far more effective to first call someone who has advertised in the paper than to simply send a letter and resume. You can come to know people through the Yellow Pages, personal referrals, and other ways. You might not have known them yesterday, but you can get to know them today.

So I'll assume you have made some sort of personal contact before sending your resume. Within this assumption are hundreds of possible situations, but I will review the most important ones in the following box and let you adapt your approach to your own situation.

The Four Types of Cover Letters to People You Know

You will be in one of four basic situations when you send cover letters to people you know. Each situation requires a different approach.

1. **An interview is scheduled and a specific job opening might interest you.** In this case, you have already arranged an interview for a job opening that interests you. The cover letter should provide details of your experience that relate to the specific job.

2. **An interview is scheduled but no specific job is available.** In essence, you will send this letter for an interview with an employer who does not have a specific opening for you now but who might in the future. This is fertile ground for finding job leads where no one else might be looking.

3. **An interview has taken place.** Many people overlook the importance of sending a letter after an interview. This is a time to say that you want the job (if that is the case, your letter should say so) and add any details on why you think you can do the job well.

4. **No interview is scheduled yet.** In some situations you just can't arrange an interview before you send a resume and cover letter. For example, you might be trying to see a person whose name was given to you by a friend, but that person is on vacation. In these cases, sending a good cover letter and resume will allow any later contacts to be more effective.

I provide sample cover letters for each situation later in this chapter. Look at the samples for each type of cover letter and see how, in most cases, they assume that personal contact was made before the resume was sent.

The following are sample cover letters for the most common situations. Note that they use different formats and styles to show you the range of styles that are appropriate. Each addresses a different situation, and each incorporates all of the cover letter writing guidelines presented earlier in this chapter.

Sample Cover Letter: Pre-Interview, for a Specific Job Opening

Comments: This writer called first and arranged an interview, which is the best approach of all. Note how this new graduate included a specific example of how he saved money for a business by changing its procedures. Although it is not clear from the letter, he gained his experience with people by working as a waiter. Note also how he included skills such as "hard worker" and "deadline pressures."

Richard Swanson
113 South Meridian
Greenwich, Connecticut 11721

March 10, XXXX

Mr. William Hines
New England Power and Light Company
604 Waterway Boulevard
Darien, Connecticut 11716

Dear Mr. Hines:

I am following up on the brief chat we had today by phone. After getting the details on the position you have open, I am certain that it is the kind of job I have been looking for. A copy of my resume is enclosed providing more details of my background. I hope you have a chance to review it before we meet next week.

My special interest has long been in the large-volume order processing systems that your organization has developed so well. While in school, I researched the flow of order processing work for a large corporation as part of a class assignment. With some simple and inexpensive procedural changes I recommended, check-processing time was reduced by an average of three days. For the number of checks and dollars involved, this one change resulted in an estimated increase in interest revenues of over $35,000 per year.

While I have recently graduated from business school, I have considerable experience for a person of my age. I have worked in a variety of jobs dealing with large numbers of people and deadline pressures. My studies have also been far more "hands-on" and practical than those of most schools, so I have a good working knowledge of current business systems and procedures. This includes a good understanding of various computer spreadsheet and applications programs, the use of automation, and experience with cutting costs and increasing profits. I am also a hard worker and realize I will need to apply myself to get established in my career.

I am most interested in the position you have available and am excited about the potential it offers. I look forward to seeing you next week. If you need to reach me before then, you can call me at (973) 299-3643 or email me at rswanson@msn.net.

Sincerely,

Richard Swanson

Sample Cover Letter: Pre-Interview, No Specific Job Opening

Comments: This letter indicates that the writer first called and set up an interview as the result of someone else's tip. The writer explains why she is moving to the city and asks for help in making contacts there. Although no job opening exists here, she is wise in assuming that there might be one in the future. Even if this is not the case, she asks the employer to think of others who might have a position for someone with her skills. Assuming that the interview goes well and the employer gives her names of others to call, she can then follow up with them.

ANNE MARIE ROAD

February 20, XXXX

Ms. Francine Cook
Park-Halsey Corporation
5413 Armstrong Drive
Minneapolis, Minnesota 56317

Dear Ms. Cook:

When Steve Marks suggested I call you, I had no idea you would be so helpful. I've already followed up with several of the suggestions you made and am now looking forward to meeting with you next Tuesday. The resume I've enclosed is to give you a better sense of my qualifications. Perhaps it will help you think of other organizations that may be interested in my background.

The resume does not say why I've moved to Minneapolis and you may find that of interest. My spouse and I visited the city several years ago and thought it a good place to live. He has obtained a very good position here and, based on that, we decided it was time to commit ourselves to a move.

As you can see from my work experience, I tend to stay on and move up in jobs, so I now want to research the job opportunities here more carefully before making a commitment. Your help in this task is greatly appreciated.

Feel free to contact me at (834) 264-3720 if you have any questions; otherwise, I look forward to meeting with you next Tuesday.

Sincerely,

Anne Marie Road

616 KINGS WAY ROAD
MINNEAPOLIS, MINNESOTA 54312
(834) 264-3720

Sample Cover Letter: After an Interview

Comments: This letter shows how you might follow up after an interview and make a pitch for solving a problem—even when no job opening formally exists. In this example, the writer suggests that she can use her skills to solve a specific problem she uncovered during her conversation with the employer. Although it never occurs to many job seekers to set up an interview where there appears to be no job opening, employers do create jobs as a result of such interviews.

Sandra A. Zaremba

115 South Hawthorn Drive
Dunwoody, Georgia 21599

April 10, XXXX

Ms. Christine Massey
Import Distributors, Inc.
417 East Main Street
Atlanta, Georgia 21649

Dear Ms. Massey:

I know you have a busy schedule so I was pleasantly surprised when you arranged a time for me to see you. While you don't have a position open now, your organization is just the sort of place I would like to work. As we discussed, I like to be busy with a variety of duties and the active pace I saw at your company is what I seek.

Your ideas on increasing business sound creative. I've thought about the customer service problem and would like to discuss a possible solution. It would involve the use of a simple system of color-coded files that would prioritize correspondence to give older requests priority status. The handling of complaints could also be speeded up through the use of simple form letters similar to those you mentioned. I have some thoughts on how this might be done, too, and I will work out a draft of procedures and sample letters if you are interested. It can be done on the computers your staff already uses and would not require any additional cost to implement.

Whether or not you have a position for me in the future, I appreciate the time you have given me. An extra copy of my resume is enclosed for your files—or to pass on to someone else.

Let me know if you want to discuss the ideas I presented earlier in this letter. I can be reached at any time on my cell phone at (942) 267-1103. I will call you next week, as you suggested, to keep you informed of my progress.

Sincerely,

Sandra A. Zaremba

Sample Cover Letter: No Interview Is Scheduled

Comments: This letter explains why the person is looking for a job as well as presents additional information that would not normally be included in a resume. Note that the writer got the employer's name from the membership list of a professional organization, which is one excellent source of job leads. Also note that the writer states that he will call again to arrange an appointment. Although this letter is assertive and might turn off some employers, many others would be impressed with the writer's assertiveness and would be willing to see him when he finally reaches them.

8661 Bay Drive
Tempe, Arizona 27317
827-994-2765

Justin Moore

January 5, XXXX

Ms. Doris Michaelmann
Michaelmann Clothing
8661 Parkway Boulevard
Phoenix, Arizona 27312

Dear Ms. Michaelmann:

As you may know, I phoned you several times over the past week while you were in meetings. I hope that you received the messages. Since I did not want to delay contacting you, I decided to write. I got your name from the American Retail Clothing Association membership list. I am a member of this group and wanted to contact local members to ask their help in locating a suitable position. I realize that you probably don't have an available position for someone with my skills, but I ask you to do two things on my behalf.

First, I ask that you consider seeing me at your convenience within the next few weeks. Though you may not have a position available for me, you may be able to assist me in other ways. And, of course, I would appreciate any consideration for future openings. Second, you may know of others who have job openings now or might possibly have them in the future.

While I realize that this is an unusual request and that you are quite busy, I do plan on staying in the retail clothing business in this area for some time and would appreciate any assistance you can give me in my search for a new job.

My resume is attached for your information along with a "JIST Card" that summarizes my background. As you probably know, Allied Tailoring has closed and I stayed on to shut things down in an orderly way. Despite their regrettable business failure, I was one of those responsible for Allied's enormous sales increases over the past decade and have substantial experience to bring to any growing retail clothing concern, such as I hear yours is.

I will contact you next week and arrange a time that is good for us both. Please feel free to contact me at any time regarding this matter. You can reach me on my cell phone at 827-994-2765.

Sincerely,

Justin Moore

Writing Cover Letters to People You Don't Know

If it is not practical to directly contact a prospective employer by phone or some other method, it is acceptable to send a resume and cover letter. This approach makes sense in some situations, such as if you are moving to a distant location or responding to a blind ad that offers only a post-office box number.

I do not recommend the approach of sending out "To Whom It May Concern" letters by the basketful. However, sending an unsolicited resume can make sense in some situations, and there are ways to modify this "shotgun" approach to be more effective. Try to find something you have in common with the person you are contacting. By mentioning this link, your letter then becomes a very personal request for assistance. Look at the two letters that follow for ideas.

Sample Cover Letter: Response to a Want Ad

Comments: Responding to a want ad puts you in direct competition with the many others who will read the same ad, so the odds are not good that this letter would get a response. The fact that the writer does not yet live in the area is another negative. Still, I believe that you should follow up on any legitimate lead you find. In this case, someone who is available to interview right away will likely fill the position. But a chance exists that, with good follow-up, another position will become available. Or the employer might be able to give the writer the names of others to contact.

John Andrews

January 17, XXXX

The Morning Sun
Box N4317
2 Early Drive
Toronto, Ontario R5C 153

Re: Receptionist/Bookkeeper Position

As I plan on relocating to Toronto, your advertisement for a Receptionist/Bookkeeper caught my attention. Your ad stated yours is a small office and that is precisely what I am looking for. I like dealing with people, and in a previous position, had over 5,000 customer contacts a month. With that experience, I have learned to handle things quickly and pleasantly.

The varied activities in a position combining bookkeeping and reception sound very interesting. I have received formal training in accounting methods and am familiar with accounts receivable, accounts payable, and general ledger posting. I am familiar with several computerized accounting programs and can quickly learn any others that you may be using.

My resume is enclosed for your consideration. Note that I went to school in Toronto and I plan on returning there soon to establish my career. Several members of my family also live there and I have provided their local phone number, should you wish to contact me. Please contact that number as soon as possible, since I plan on being in Toronto in the near future and would like to speak with you about this or future positions with your company. I will call you in the next few weeks to set up an appointment should I not hear from you before then.

Thank you in advance for your consideration in this matter.

Sincerely,

John Andrews

12 Lake Street
Chicago, Illinois 60631
587.488.3876
johnandrews@cincore.com

P.S. You can reach me via email at johnandrews@cincore.com or leave a phone message at 587.488.3876.

Sample Cover Letter: Unsolicited Resume Sent to Obtain an Interview

Comments: This is another example of a person conducting a long-distance job search using names obtained from a professional association. This letter also explains why he is leaving his old job and includes positive information regarding his references and skills that would not normally be found in a resume. John asks for an interview even though there might not be any jobs open now, and also asks for names of others to contact.

July 10, XXXX

Mr. Paul Resley
Operations Manager
Rollem Trucking Co.
1-70 Freeway Drive
Kansas City, Missouri 78401

Mr. Resley:

I obtained your name from the membership directory of the Affiliated Trucking Association. I have been a member for over 10 years, and I am very active in the Southeast Region. The reason I am writing is to ask for your help. The firm I had been employed with has been bought by a larger corporation. The operations here have been disbanded, leaving me unemployed.

While I like where I live, I know that finding a position at the level of responsibility I seek may require a move. As a center of the transportation business, your city is one I have targeted for special attention. A copy of my resume is enclosed for your use. I'd like you to review it and consider where a person with my background would get a good reception in Kansas City. Perhaps you could think of a specific person for me to contact?

I have specialized in fast-growing organizations or ones that have experienced rapid change. My particular strength is in bringing things under control, then increasing profits. While my resume does not state this, I have excellent references from my former employer and would have stayed if a similar position existed at its new location.

As a member of the association, I hoped that you would provide some special attention to my request for assistance. I plan on coming to Kansas City on a job-hunting trip within the next six weeks. Prior to my trip I will call you for advice on who I might contact for interviews. Even if they have no jobs open for me now, perhaps they will know of someone else who does.

My enclosed resume lists my phone number and other contact information should you want to reach me before I call you. Thanks in advance for your help on this.

Sincerely,

John B. Goode
Treasurer, Southeast Region
Affiliated Trucking Association

John B. Goode

312 Smokie Way   Nashville, Tennessee 31201

Additional Sample Cover Letters

I've included some additional cover letters that address a variety of situations. Most do not include graphics and were formatted in letter templates that come with well-known word processing programs. Although the formats are not fancy, they are acceptable and quick.

The letters from Patricia Dugan and Douglas Parker came from Dave Swanson's book, *The Resume Solution*. I've also included letters by John Harris, John Trost, and Richard Peterson that feature interesting design elements and formats. Professional resume writer Rafael Santiago in Papillion, Nebraska, provided these letters.

I hope that these samples give you ideas on writing your own cover letters. Once you get the hang of it, you should be able to write a simple cover letter in about 15 minutes. Just keep in mind that the best cover letter is one that you send after setting up an interview. Anything else is just second best, at best.

Figure 4-7: No Interview Is Scheduled

947 Cherry Street
Middleville, Ohio 01234

October 22, XXXX

Mr. Alfred E. Newman, President
Alnew Consolidated Stores, Inc.
1 Newman Place
New City, OK 03000

Dear Mr. Newman:

I am interested in the position of national sales director, which you recently advertised in the *Retail Sales and Marketing* newsletter.

I am very familiar with your company's innovative marketing techniques as well as your enlightened policy in promoting and selling environmentally sound merchandise nationwide. I have been active for some time now in environmental protection projects, both as a representative of my current employer and on my own. I recently successfully introduced a new line of kitchen products that exceeds federal standards, is environmentally safe, and is selling well.

The enclosed resume outlines my experience and skills in both sales and marketing in the retail field. I would like to meet with you to discuss how my skills would benefit Alnew Consolidated Stores. I will contact you soon to request an interview for current or future positions and may be reached at (513) 987-6543.

Thank you for your time and consideration.

Sincerely,

Robin Redding

Figure 4-8: Pre-Interview, No Specific Job Opening

Lisa Marie Farkel

3321 Haverford Road
Baldwin, North Carolina
12294

Email: lfarkel@dotcom.net
Phone: 400-541-0877
FAX: 400-541-0988

March 15, XXXX

Mr. Howard Duty
WXLC TV
10212 North Oxford Avenue
Halstead, South Carolina 12456

Dear Mr. Duty:

Thank you for agreeing to meet with me at 3 p.m. on March 23rd to talk about job opportunities for broadcast technicians. Although I understand that you have no openings right now, I'm enclosing my resume to give you some information about my training and background.

You will see that I have worked on both up-to-date and as well as older equipment. Working part time for a small station, I've learned to monitor, adjust, and repair a variety of equipment including both the newer automated and computerized items as well as the older ones. Keeping a mix of older and newer equipment working smoothly has required me to learn many things and has been an invaluable experience. At Halstead Junior College, I have become the person to call if the new, state-of-the-art audio and video equipment does not perform as it should.

I look forward to graduating and devoting all my time and energy to my career. Your help is greatly appreciated, particularly your invitation to spend more time observing field operations during your live election coverage.

Sincerely,

Lisa Marie Farkel

P.S. I found your Web site and was *very* impressed that you did most of the work on it. You may be interested to know that I have created a Web site for our college TV station. If you have time, you can find it at halstead.edu/WNCSTV —I'd like your feedback!

Enclosure: resume

Figure 4-9: No Interview Is Scheduled

6345 Highland Boulevard
Minneapolis, Minnesota

June 28, XXXX

Mr. James A. Blackwell
Vice President, Engineering
Acme Revolving Door Company
New Brunswick, Pennsylvania 21990

Dear Mr. Blackwell:

I graduated from the University of Minnesota this spring with a 3.66 grade average and a Bachelor of Science Degree in Mechanical Engineering.

Your company has been highly recommended to me by my uncle, John Blair, the Pennsylvania District Governor for Rotary, International. He has appreciated your friendship and business relationship over the years and has advised me to forward my resume. My own reading in business publications has kept me aware of the new products that Acme has marketed. Also, I recently visited your excellent Web site and was impressed with the variety of materials you produce.

My objective is to design mechanical parts for a privately owned company that enjoys an excellent reputation and that conducts business internationally.

I hope that I may take the liberty of calling your office to see if we might meet to discuss possible opportunities with Acme. I plan to be in Pennsylvania toward the end of next month, and this might provide a convenient time to meet, if your schedule permits.

Sincerely,

Patricia Dugan
(612) 555-3445

Figure 4-10: Pre-Interview, for a Specific Job Opening

1768 South Carrollton Street
Nashville, Tennessee 96050
May 26, XXXX

Ms. Karen Miller
Office Manager
Lendon, Lendon, and Sears
Suite 101, Landmark Building
Summit, New Jersey 11736

Dear Ms. Miller:

Enclosed is a copy of my resume that describes my work experience as a legal assistant. I hope this information will be helpful as background for our interview next Monday at 4 p.m.

I appreciate your taking time to describe your requirements so fully. This sounds like a position that could develop into a satisfying career. And my training in accounting—along with experience using a variety of computer programs—seems to match your needs.

Lendon, Lendon, and Sears is a highly respected name in New Jersey. I am excited about this opportunity and I look forward to meeting with you.

Sincerely,

Richard Wittenberg

Sample Cover Letter: No Interview Is Scheduled

ALBAROSA BARTON
12603 SOUTH 33rd STREET
OMAHA, NEBRASKA 68123
PHONE (402) 292-9052
FAX (402) 393-0099
EMAIL ALBAROSA@OFCORPS.COM

March 30, XXXX

YALE BUSINESS SERVICES
Alexander Bell, Director of Human Resources
1005 Denver Street, Suite 1
Bellevue, Nebraska 68005-4145

Dear Mr. Bell:

I am enclosing a copy of my resume for your consideration and would like to call your attention to the skills and achievements in my background that are most relevant.

I am an achiever, with four years of experience as a highly successful administrator. I've always set high standards and consistently achieved my goals. I've served in the United States Air Force since February 1998 as an Administrative Specialist/Assistant. I acquired my training through the excellent programs the Air Force provides. I am highly motivated and would be a dynamic administrator for whatever company I represent.

I am confident in my administrative abilities and have already proven myself in the areas of office administration and customer relations.

I look forward to hearing from you soon and having the opportunity to discuss your needs and plans.

Cordially,

ALBAROSA BARTON

Figure 4-12: No Interview Is Scheduled

4550 Parrier Street
Espinosa, California 44478

August 11, XXXX

Mr. Craig Schmidt
District Manager
Desert Chicken Shops
Post Office Box 6230
Los Angeles, California 98865

Dear Mr. Schmidt:

My resume (enclosed) outlines my four years of successful experience as a fast food manager with a nationwide network of restaurants. I graduated from a Restaurant Management curriculum at Harman University with a 3.75 GPA in 1998.

I have been impressed with the rapid growth and exceptional quality of product and service for which Desert Chicken has become well known. This is the kind of organization I hope to work for now.

My experience includes positions as cook, night manager, assistant manager, and manager for my current employer.

I will call your office in a few days to see if we might schedule a convenient time to meet and discuss some areas of mutual interest.

Thanks very much for your consideration.

Sincerely,

Douglas Parker

Enclosure

Figure 4-13: No Interview Is Scheduled

Apartment A35
4085 Larchmont Road
Seattle, Washington 97033

September 1, XXXX

The Seattle News
Box N9142
1414 East New York Street
Seattle, Washington 97002

Your advertisement for an Administrative Assistant could have been written with me in mind. I have had three years' experience in a busy office where time management, communication skills, and ability to deal with all kinds of people are vital.

Directing support staff, writing customer service letters, and preparing monthly, quarterly, and yearly sales reports are my responsibilities. I regularly use computer software packages to track and maintain our sales revenues and customer mailing lists. I am proficient in word processing, database, and spreadsheet software on both Mac- and PC-based computers and frequently use the Internet for research. My communication skills are excellent, and I can work on multiple tasks and still meet deadlines.

For your consideration, I have enclosed a resume that more completely describes my education and experience. I look forward to meeting with you soon.

Sincerely,

Susan Deming

(555) 555-3221 cell phone
susandeming@email.net

The Hardworking JIST Card

JIST Cards are a job search tool that gets results. I developed JIST Cards in the early 1970s, almost by accident. I was surprised by the positive employer reaction but paid attention and developed them further. Over the years, I have seen them in every imaginable format, and forms of JIST Cards are now being used on the Internet, in personal video interviews, and in other electronic media.

Think of a JIST Card as a Very Small Resume

A JIST Card is carefully constructed to contain all the essential information most employers want to know in a very short format:

- Name, phone number, and e-mail address
- The type of position you seek
- Your experience, education, and training
- Key job-related skills, performance, and results
- Your good-worker traits
- Any special conditions you are willing to work under (optional)

A JIST Card typically uses a 3×5-inch card format but has been designed into many other sizes and formats, such as a folded business card. It can be as simple as handwritten or done with graphics and on special papers. You should create JIST Cards in addition to a resume because you will use your JIST Cards in a different way.

JIST Cards Get Results

What matters is what JIST Cards accomplish—they get results. In my surveys of employers, more than 90 percent of employers form a positive impression of the JIST Card's writer within 30 seconds. More amazing is that about 80 percent of employers say they would be willing to interview the person behind the JIST Card, even if they did not have a job opening at the time.

How You Can Use Them

You can use a JIST Card in many ways, including the following:

- Attached to your resume or application

- Enclosed in a thank-you note

- Given to your friends, relatives, and other contacts—so that they can give them to other people

- Sent out to everyone who graduated from your school or who are members of a professional association

- Put on car windshields

- Posted on the supermarket bulletin board

- On the Internet, in addition to resume content

I'm not kidding about finding JIST Cards on windshields or bulletin boards. I've seen them used in these ways and hear about more ways people are using them all the time.

JIST Card Paper and Format Tips

Many office-supply stores have perforated light card stock sheets that you can run through your computer printer. You can then tear them apart into 3×5-inch cards. Many word-processing programs have templates that allow you to format a 3×5-inch card size. You can also use regular size paper, print several cards on a sheet, and cut it to the size you need. Print shops can also photocopy or print them in the size you need. Get a few hundred at a time. They are cheap, and the point is to get lots of them in circulation.

Sample JIST Cards

The following sample JIST Cards use a plain format, but you can make them as fancy as you want. So be creative. Look over the examples to see how they are constructed. Some are for entry-level jobs and some are for more advanced ones.

Sandy Nolan

Position: General Office/Clerical

Message: (512) 232-9213

More than two years of work experience plus one year of training in office practices. Type 55 wpm, trained in word processing, post general ledger, interpersonal skills, and get along with most people. Can meet deadlines and handle pressure well.

Willing to work any hours

Organized, honest, reliable, and hardworking

Joyce Hua   Home: (214) 173-1659

Message: (214) 274-1436   E-mail: jhua@yahoo.com

Position: Programming/Systems Analyst

More than 10 years of combined education and experience in data processing and related fields. Competent programming in Visual Basic, C, C++, FORTRAN, Java, and database management. Extensive PC network applications experience. Have supervised a staff as large as seven on special projects and have a record of meeting deadlines. Operations background in management, sales, and accounting.

Desire career-oriented position; will relocate

Dedicated, self-starter, creative problem solver

Paul Thomas   Home: (301) 681-3922
                                    Message: (301) 681-6966
                                    Cell phone: (301) 927-9856

Position: Research Chemist, Research Management
                 in a small-to-medium–sized company

Ph.D. in biochemistry plus more than 15 years of work experience. Developed
and patented various processes with current commercial applications worth
many millions of dollars. Experienced with all phases of lab work with an
emphasis on chromatography, isolation, and purification of organic and
biochemical compounds. Specialized in practical pharmaceutical and agricultural
applications of chemical research. Have teaching, supervision, and project-
management experience.

Married more than 15 years, stable work history, results and task oriented,
ambitious, and willing to relocate

Richard Straightarrow   **Home: (602) 253-9678**
                                    Message: (602) 257-6643

Objective: Electronics installation, maintenance, and sales

Four years of work experience plus two-year AA degree in Electronics
Engineering Technology. Managed a $360,000/year business while going
to school full time, with grades in the top 25%. Familiar with all major
electronic diagnostic and repair equipment. Hands-on experience with
medical, consumer, communication, and industrial electronics equipment
and applications. Good problem-solving and communication skills. Customer-
service oriented.

Willing to do what it takes to get the job done

Self motivated, dependable, learn quickly

Juanita Rodriguez   Message: (639) 361-1754

Position: Warehouse Management

Six years of experience plus two years of formal business course work. Have supervised a staff as large as 16 people and warehousing operations covering more than two acres and valued at over $14,000,000. Automated inventory operations resulting in a 30% increase in turnover and estimated annual savings of more than $250,000. Working knowledge of accounting, computer systems, time & motion studies, and advanced inventory-management systems.

Will work any hours

Responsible, hardworking, and can solve problems

Deborah Levy   Home: (213) 432-8064
                                        Pager: (212) 876-9487

Position: Hotel Management

Four years of experience in sales, catering, and accounting in a 300-room hotel. Associate degree in Hotel Management plus one year with the Boileau Culinary Institute. Doubled revenues from meetings and conferences. Increased dining room and bar revenues by 44%. Have been commended for improving staff productivity and courtesy. I approach my work with industry, imagination, and creative problem-solving skills.

Enthusiastic, well-organized, detail-oriented

Jonathan Michael   Cell phone: (614) 788-2434
                                        E-mail: jonn@pike.org

Objective: Management

More than 7 years of management experience plus a BS degree in business. Managed budgets as large as $10 million. Experienced in cost control and reduction, cutting more than 20% of overhead while business increased more than 30%. Good organizer and problem solver. Excellent communication skills.

Prefer responsible position in a medium-to-large business

Cope well with deadline pressure, seek challenge, flexible

Thank-You Notes

Although resumes and cover letters get the attention, thank-you notes often get results. That's right. Sending thank-you notes makes both good manners and good job search sense. When used properly, thank-you notes can help you create a positive impression with employers that more formal correspondence often can't.

Three Times When You Should Definitely Send Thank-You Notes—and Why

Thank-you notes have a more intimate and friendly social tradition than formal and manipulative business correspondence. I think that is one reason they work so well—people respond to those who show good manners and say thank you. Here are some situations when you should use them, along with some sample notes for each situation.

1. Before an Interview

In some situations, you can send a less formal note before an interview. For example, you can simply thank someone for being willing to see you. Depending on the situation, enclosing a resume could be a bit inappropriate. Remember, this is supposed to be sincere thanks for help and not an assertive business situation.

Sample Thank-You Note 1

April 5, XXXX

Ms. Kijek,

Thanks so much for your willingness to see me next Wednesday at 9 a.m. I know that I am one of many who are interested in working with your organization. I appreciate the opportunity to meet you and learn more about the position.

I've enclosed a JIST Card that presents the basics of my skills for this job and will bring my resume to the interview. Please call me if you have any questions at all.

Sincerely,

Bruce Vernon

2. After an Interview

One of the best times to send a thank-you note is right after an interview. Here are several reasons why:

- Doing so creates a positive impression. The employer will assume you have good follow-up skills—and good manners.

- It creates yet another opportunity for you to remain in the employer's consciousness at an important time.

- If they buried, passed along, or otherwise lost your resume and previous correspondence, a thank-you note and corresponding JIST Card provide one more chance for employers to find your number and call you.

TIP: *Enclose a JIST Card with each thank-you note you send. They fit well into an envelope and provide key information an employer can use to contact you. JIST Cards also list key skills and other credentials that will help you create a good impression. And the employer could always forward the card to someone who might have a job opening for you.*

For these reasons, I suggest you send a thank-you note right after the interview and certainly within 24 hours, when you are freshest in the employer's mind. The following is an example of such a note.

Sample Thank-You Note 2

August 11, XXXX

Dear Mr. O'Beel,

Thank you for the opportunity to interview for the position available in your production department. I want you to know that this is the sort of job I have been looking for and that I am enthusiastic about the possibility of working for you.

I believe that I have both the experience and skills to fit nicely into your organization and to be productive quickly.

Thanks again for the interview; I enjoyed the visit.

Sara Smith

(505) 665-0090

3. Whenever Anyone Helps You in Your Job Search

Send a thank-you note to anyone who helps you during your job search. This includes those who give you referrals, people who provide advice, or simply those who are supportive during your search. I suggest you routinely enclose one or more JIST Cards in these notes because recipients can give them to others who might be in a better position to help you.

Sample Thank-You Note 3

October 31, XXXX

Debbie Childs
2234 Riverbed Avenue
Philadelphia, PA 17963

Ms. Helen A. Colcord
Henderson and Associates, Inc.
1801 Washington Blvd., Suite 1201
Philadelphia, PA 17963

Dear Ms. Colcord,

Thank you for sharing your time with me so generously yesterday. I really appreciated talking to you about your career field.

The information you shared with me increased my desire to work in such an area. Your advice has already proven helpful—I have an appointment to meet with Robert Hopper on Friday.

In case you think of someone else who might need a person like me, I'm enclosing another resume and JIST Card.

Sincerely,

Debbie Childs

Seven Quick Tips for Writing Thank-You Notes

Here are some brief tips to help you write your thank-you notes.

1. Use Quality Paper and Envelopes

Use good quality notepaper with matching envelopes. Most stationery stores have thank-you note cards and envelopes in a variety of styles. Select a note that is simple and professional—avoid cute graphics and sayings. A simple "Thank You" on the front will do. For a professional look, match your resume and thank-you note papers by getting them at the same time. I suggest off-white and buff colors.

2. Handwritten or Typed Is Acceptable

Traditionally, thank-you notes are handwritten. If your handwriting is good, it is perfectly acceptable to write them. If not, they can be word-processed.

3. Use a Formal Salutation

Unless you know the person you are thanking, don't use a first name. Write "Dear Ms. Pam Smith," "Ms. Smith," or "Dear Ms. Smith" rather than the less formal "Dear Pam." Include the date.

4. Keep the Note Informal and Friendly

Keep your note short and friendly. This is not the place to write "The reason you should hire me is…." Remember, the note is a thank-you for what *someone else* did, not a hard-sell pitch for what *you* want. And make sure it doesn't sound like a form letter.

As appropriate, be specific about when you will next contact the person. If you plan to meet soon, still send a note saying you look forward to the meeting and say thank you for the appointment. And make sure that you include something to remind the employer of who you are and how to reach you because your name alone might not be enough to be remembered.

5. Sign It

Sign your first and last name. Avoid initials and make your signature legible.

6. Send It Right Away

Write and send your note no later than 24 hours after you make your contact. Ideally, you should write it immediately after the contact, while the details are fresh in your mind.

7. Enclose a JIST Card

Depending on the situation, a JIST Card is often the ideal enclosure to include with a thank-you note. It's small, soft sell, and provides your phone number, should the employer want to reach you. It is both a reminder of you, should any jobs open up, and a tool to pass along to someone else. Make sure your thank-you notes and envelopes are big enough to enclose an unfolded JIST Card.

Chapter 5

Use Your Resume on the Internet

A lthough the Internet has helped many people find job leads, far more have been disappointed. The problem is that many job seekers assume they can simply put resumes in Internet resume databases, and employers will line up to hire them. It sometimes happens this way, but not often. This is the same negative experience that people have when sending lots of unsolicited resumes to personnel offices—a hopeful but mostly ineffective approach that was around long before computers.

As with sending out many unsolicited resumes, putting your resume on the Internet is a passive approach that is unlikely to work well for you. Use the Internet smartly in your job search, but also plan to use other offline techniques, including direct contacts with employers.

Multiple Ways to Use the Internet in Your Job Search

Job seeking on the Internet involves more than simply posting your resume on one or more resume database sites or contacting employers by e-mail. Here are some other ways the Internet can help you in your job search:

- **Employer Web sites.** Many employers have Web sites that include career information and a process for applying to current job openings. Checking out employee *blogs* (short for *Web logs*, or online journals) can give you a sense of the corporate culture. Some sites allow you to interact with staff online or via e-mail to get answers to questions about working there.

- **Inside information.** You can use search engines such as Google and other Web sites to find information on a specific employer or industry (for example, see www.vault.com, www.wetfeet.com, and www.jobster.com); get job descriptions that list skills and requirements to emphasize in interviews and on your resume (for example, see www.careeroink.com); find career counseling and job search advice (for example, see www.certifiedcareercoaches.com); and look up almost anything else you need related to your job search.

- **Job boards.** Large national sites such as Monster and HotJobs let you search for openings based on specific criteria.

- **Specialty sites.** You can find Web sites that specialize in the jobs that interest you (for example, www.dice.com for technology careers). Many have job postings, useful information, and access to people in the know. Also, many geographic-specific sites for cities and towns list local openings.

- **Networking.** Create a profile on business networking Web sites like LinkedIn, Rzye, and ecademy to organize your existing network and make new contacts for career research. When you are able to see the contacts that your contacts have, you can better tell them how they can be of help.

For suggestions on the best sites to help you in your job search, see the end of this chapter; for even more help, see the book *Best Career and Education Web Sites* from JIST.

Adapting Your Resume for Electronic Use

When you post your resume to an online resume database such as Monster, it is stored as a text file with no graphics or other fancy formatting, so that it takes up less space and any type of computer can read it. Employers search these text files for keywords that match their requirements for the jobs they have open. Also, employers prefer resumes in electronic form to avoid having to scan them before adding them to their own searchable databases.

What this means is that your resume's carefully done format-and-design elements get stripped out in these processes. Plus, scanning can introduce text errors and odd formatting due to the imperfect science of scanning technology. So, you are better off making the modifications yourself before distributing your resume online.

Sample Text-Only Resume, with All Graphics and Formatting Removed

Look at the sample resume that follows, adapted from one by Susan Britton Whitcomb in _Résumé Magic_ (2003, JIST Publishing). This resume has had all formatting and graphic elements removed for submission in electronic or scannable form. It has the following features:

- No graphics
- No lines (it uses equal signs instead)
- No bold, italic, or other text variations
- Only one easy-to-scan font (Courier in this case)
- No tab indents
- No line or paragraph indents

Yes, this resume looks boring, but it has the advantage of being universally accepted into company databases or online job boards.

Figure 5-1: A Plain-Text Resume

```
AMY RICCIUTTI
Greenville, ME
(203) 433-3322
aricciutti@aol.com

PROFESSIONAL EXPERIENCE
=========================================================================

ROCKWOOD INSURANCE, Augusta, ME
10/00-Present

Independent agency specializing in commercial coverage for
transportation and lumber industries.

Underwriting Manager ...

Recruited by partner / sales manager to manage underwriting in support of
aggressive expansion / business development campaign.  Liaison to five
agents and some 50 companies.  Underwrite $6 million in renewal coverage
and $200,000 in new business on a priority basis (commercial and
personal lines).  Collaborate with agents to protect loss ratios.
Aggressively process submissions to meet critical deadlines and offer
better premiums to customers.

*** Contributions ***

+ Developed focus and structure for newly created position; established
underwriting and customer service infrastructure to support a projected
$500,000 increase in annual revenue.

+ Achieved new agency record for retaining renewal accounts.

+ Earned accolades from insurance companies for having "most complete
submissions."

+ Trained two Customer Representatives, equipping them with technical
knowledge to service complete accounts.

+ Designed and introduced Quote Worksheet and Agent Checklist to
standardize and streamline underwriting.

+ Diplomatically mitigated circumstances involving premium increases and
noncoverage of claims.

COAST INSURANCE SERVICES, Brunswick, ME
1995-2000

Senior Customer Service Representative ...

Accountable for policy maintenance, renewal retention, new business
submissions, claims, CSR training, and liaison work for independent
agency with $7 million in premiums.
```

```
*** Contributions ***

+ Assisted with AMS Novell network upgrade (resident expert for
software installation, troubleshooting).

+ Took on several new books of business during tenure without
need for additional support staff.


SUPPORTING SKILLS, INFORMATION
============================================================================

    *** Education *** INS 21 (Principles of Insurance).  INS 23
    (Commercial Principles of Insurance). Personal Lines
    (Property and Auto). Commercial Lines (Property). E&O
    Coverage. Employee Practices Liability. Property & Casualty
    Agent (# 760923)

    *** Computer *** Windows 3.1. Windows 95 and 98. MS Works.
    MS Office. WordPerfect. AMS Novell. DOS and UNIX-based
    programs. Redshaw. OIS and FSC Rating Systems. PS4 Proposal
    Systems.

    *** Affiliations *** National Association of Insurance Women.
    National Association of Female Executives. Volunteer, Marine
    Mammal Center.
```

Converting Your Resume to Electronic Format

You can easily take your existing resume and reformat it for electronic submission. Here are some quick guidelines to do so:

- Copy and paste your resume text into a new file in your word processor.

- Eliminate graphic elements such as lines or images.

- Set the margins to no more than 65 characters wide.

- Use an easy-to-scan type font, such as Courier or Times New Roman. Eliminate bold, italic, and other styles.

- Introduce major sections with words in all uppercase letters, rather than in bold or a different style.

- Keep all text left-aligned.

- Use standard keyboard characters such as the asterisk in place of bullets.

- Instead of using the tab key or paragraph indents, use the space key to indent.

When you're done, click the File menu and the Save As command. Then select the Plain Text, ASCII (American Standard Code for Information Interchange), or Text Only option from the Save As Type box. Then name the file and click Save or OK. Then reopen the file to see how it looks. Make any additional format changes as needed.

Close the document and reopen it in a text editor, such as Notepad or TextEdit (Mac OS X), just to double-check that all of the characters have been converted correctly.

Now you are ready to e-mail your resume. Always paste the text/ASCII version into the body of your e-mail message to ensure receipt. If the employer hasn't banned attachments, also attach your resume as a PDF file. These files preserve your formatting and allow hiring managers to print an attractive version of your resume. If you are submitting the resume to an Internet database, follow the site's instructions on how to submit your resume.

The Importance of Keywords

Creating an electronic resume is more involved than just putting it into a plain format. Employers look for qualified applicants in a resume databank by searching for what are called *keywords*. Your task is to add the right keywords to your electronic resume so that your chance of being selected for appropriate jobs is increased.

> **TIP:** Most resume bank sites ask you to submit your resume by copying it from your file and pasting it into boxes on the Web site. Others ask you to upload your resume file directly to their database in plain-text format.

You will want to use keywords to make your resume match employers' job ads as closely as possible. This is especially important if you are applying to large companies, which might use a computer to search through all the resumes it receives and reject any without the right keywords—before a human being even gets to look at them! No, it doesn't seem fair, but the best way around this is to use your knowledge to get those keywords in there and to get your resume past the first cut.

Quick Tips for Selecting Keywords to Include in Your Resume

The main thing to realize when thinking about which keywords to put in your resume is that computers, although they let you do wonderful things, are just not very smart. They don't have the same power that people do to think and interpret. So your job here is to use keywords that give the computer exactly what it is looking for.

Let's say you see a job ad that asks for knowledge of Microsoft Access. You might have been working in an office for years and are familiar with Microsoft Access, Word, and all the other parts of the Microsoft Office software suite. The temptation is to just list "Microsoft Office" as a skill on your resume. The danger is that the computer might not know that Access is part of Microsoft Office and will toss out your resume. Therefore, if a job ad asks for a specific skill, use exactly the same words as in the job ad. Don't write "Microsoft Office." Instead, write "Microsoft Excel, Access, Word, and PowerPoint."

Here are some keyword tips for you to keep in mind:

- **Think like a prospective employer.** Think of the jobs you want, and then include the keywords you think an employer would use to find someone who can do what you can do.

- **Review job descriptions from major references.** Read the descriptions for the jobs you seek in major references like the *Occupational Outlook Handbook* or the *O*NET Dictionary of Occupational Titles.* These are available in both print and online formats. They will give you a variety of keywords you can use in your electronic resume.

- **Include all your important skill words.** Include the key skills you documented in chapter 3.

- **Look for additional sources of keywords to include.** You can identify keywords by reviewing the sample resumes in chapter 7, job descriptions of jobs you want, want ads, employer Web sites, job board postings, and more.

Always be as specific as possible. Read each job ad carefully, and be ready and willing to make changes to your resume when applying for different positions.

Sample Keyword Resumes

Many sample resumes in chapter 7 contain lots of keywords. These resumes were specifically designed to be easily scanned or e-mailed and most also look pretty darned good. Some provide a list of keywords in a separate section, in addition to the many keywords used throughout the resume. Look to them for inspiration on how to add more keywords to your own electronic resume.

Using the Internet to Go Beyond the Resume

Now that you've seen how you can use the Internet to uncover opportunities and effectively distribute your resume, it's also important to understand that others will be using the Internet to find and research you.

More and more, you will be googled in your job search. A recent Harris Interactive poll showed that 23 percent of people search for the names of business associates or colleagues on the Internet before meeting them, and 75 percent of recruiters are googling candidates. There are classes popping up for HR professionals on googling candidates, and peoples' Friendster profiles are even being reviewed in the recruiting process. It's clear that your online identity now has an impact on your career.

Have you googled yourself? Try typing your first and last name into Google, and then try it in quotes (such as, "Mike Farr"). When you do, you could discover one of the following:

> **TIP:** *Some job seekers have created their own interactive sites that include stunning resume graphics; video clips introducing themselves; samples of their work using photographs, video, or sound; and many other features. Unless you are looking for a job as a Web designer, this is simply too much information for most employers.*

- You don't show up at all, making potential employers wonder how important you are.

- You have a common name, and it's hard to find anything relevant to you.

- There are negative results about you (arrests, firings, or other unflattering information).

- Your personal blog or family Web site comes up high in the search results and it isn't something that you would want potential employers to find as a first impression.

- There are quite a few professionally relevant and positive results about you, but these snippets of information make it difficult to get a comprehensive picture.

- You have a Web site that comes up highly ranked in the search results and paints a clear picture of your professional self.

You can surmise from these scenarios that everything that you post online or that is written about you becomes a part of your online identity. You'll want to consider the impact, positive or negative, that a comment on someone's blog or a review on epinions.com will have.

Your Own Blog

One of the easiest and most economical ways to get an online presence that is well-designed and search-engine friendly is to create a professional *blog* (short for *Weblog*). With TypePad or Blogger, you don't have to know HTML to start posting articles about your area of expertise. Just make sure that your posts are professional and relevant to your target audience. Use this vehicle to demonstrate your knowledge, experience, and current grasp on happenings in your industry. On your blog, you can make your resume available for download (include text, Word, and PDF versions), link to other relevant sites, and include your career bio on the "about" page.

Figure 5-2 shows the blog of job seeker Nina Burokas. Nina uses a blog as part of her career strategy because it sets her apart from other job seekers, demonstrates her skills, and helps establish her personal "brand."

Figure 5-2: A Blog for Career Management

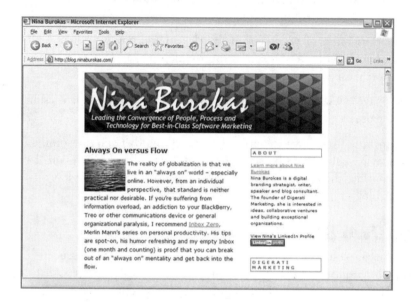

Online Career Portfolios

To go beyond the blog and create a more comprehensive picture of who you are and what you have done, you can create an online career portfolio. A Web portfolio is the traditional paper portfolio concept reinvented for the online medium with links and multimedia content. Portfolios are more than Web-based resumes in that they *must* contain tangible evidence of your past performance, including work samples, testimonials, articles, video, photographs, charts, and so on.

Providing this depth of information earlier in the career search process weeds out no-win situations and establishes virtual rapport with your interviewers. The portfolio concept also helps prove the facts on your resume because it shows and not just tells. Prospective employers and clients want to see that you have solved problems like theirs.

If you say that you have strong presentation skills, show a video clip! Articles, awards, graphs, audio references, white papers, case studies, press releases, and schedules of appearances are just some of the options you have to prove your expertise.

Figure 5-3: A Web Portfolio

Figure 5-3 shows the Web portfolio of Cindy Eng, Vice President and Editorial Director for Scholastic At Home. Says Cindy, "I landed a great new job as a direct result of a networking contact finding my Brandego portfolio and seeing that my background was a perfect match for a position that his executive recruiter was trying to fill. My Web portfolio made it easy to distribute my resume and show examples of projects during my interviews. My new colleagues told me that they were reassured by my qualifications when they googled me after the announcement of my hire. I like that when I'm googled, my portfolio is the first thing that is found."

You can check out more web portfolio examples at www.brandego.com/gallery.php.

Because most are not well executed, there has been some media backlash about the use of personal Web sites for career marketing. Many Web-based career "portfolios" do look amateurish and are a risky mix of personal information (religion, politics, lifestyle, and so on), family photos, and career-related content. What this means for you is that you have a real opportunity to stand out by getting it right.

Maybe there will come a time where the Web career portfolio is as ubiquitous as the resume; but for now, there is a lot of opportunity to stand out from your competition and be extraordinary by having one. Of course, if the design and content of your portfolio is as unique as you are, that will further differentiate you. And, like any other Web site, there has to be a compelling reason to drive traffic to it. You must go way beyond the content that is in your resume.

The bottom line? You will be googled, and when the average job lasts only about 3.5 years, it certainly makes sense to constantly foster professional visibility both online and offline.

> **TIP:** *Don't get fired for blogging! What goes in a career-management blog? There are no rules, but common sense and good writing apply. There have been cases where people have been fired for blogging about proprietary corporate information or making unflattering remarks about their work environment. Ninety percent of your posts should be relevant to your professional target audience. Because blogs are expected to reveal your personality, you should occasionally write about your interests—but only the ones that you'd also include on a resume.*

Best Resume Banks and Job Boards

These Web sites provide listings of job openings and allow you to add your resume for employers to look at. All allow you to look up job openings in a variety of useful ways including location, job type, and other criteria. Most get their fees from employers and don't charge job seekers.

BestJobsUSA.com—www.bestjobsusa.com. A nice feature here is the state site selection option, which includes a separate jobs page focused on each U.S. state. On each of these pages, you can conduct a job search in only that state and find local articles and information. You can also use the general search form to search all job listings or sign up to have matching job opportunities e-mailed to you on a regular basis.

CareerBuilder.com—www.careerbuilder.com. The same people who bring you CareerBuilder-branded help-wanted sections in Sunday papers across the country here provide a search engine to hundreds of thousands of jobs. Search by keyword, city, state, field of interest, company, industry, and/or job type; use the Job Recommendation Engine to have matching jobs e-mailed directly to your inbox.

CareerShop—www.careershop.com. CareerShop harnesses the power of the Internet to automate the job search and career-management process as much as possible for both job seekers and employers. Search for a job by category, keyword, or location; access the Ask the Career Dr. career advice; use the Personal Job Shopper to have matching jobs e-mailed to you weekly; and post your resume online.

JobBankUSA.com—www.jobbankusa.com. At JobBankUSA.com's meta-search, in addition to the jobs posted at the site itself, you can run searches in newspapers across the country or through regional job banks, other national and international job banks, and industry-specific job banks. This makes this Web site a useful one-stop shop for searching multiple resources. Use the free Resume Builder service to create an online resume, and then, for a fee, you can use ResumeBroadcaster to have your resume e-mailed to companies that match your skills.

Monster—www.monster.com. Monster, possibly the best-known careers site on the Internet, contains all the features you'd expect in a major job and resume bank. Your options here include registering to post your resume; having jobs e-mailed to you; signing up for e-mail newsletters; searching more than one million monthly job postings; applying for jobs online using the resume you posted; and finding advice, articles, and tools in an extensive online career center.

NationJob—www.nationjob.com. Search job listings by field, location, duration, educational level, and salary. Register to receive e-mail notification of new jobs matching your criteria. Research companies. Find career tools and resources. Get your degree online. Post your resume to the database. Access career articles and success stories.

NicheBoards.com—www.nicheboards.com. An alliance of 11 industry-specific job boards. Also check out the compilation of 300 niche career sites at www.quintcareers.com/indres.html.

Simply Hired—www.simplyhired.com. Simply Hired is a vertical job search engine that pulls listings from job boards, company pages, online classifieds, and other data sources, making it a veritable one-stop shop.

TheLadders.com—www.theladders.com. The most comprehensive source for six-figure executive jobs at companies of all sizes.

Vault.com—www.vault.com. Vault.com's claim to fame lies in its "insider" information on more than 3,000 companies and 70 industries. Not enough for you? Access the "Electronic Water Cooler," online company-specific message boards where you can get the lowdown from current and former employees. Of course, you can also use traditional job bank features such as searchable job postings, an online resume service, e-mail newsletters, and e-mailed job openings. One last useful feature is an extensive resume and cover letter advice section, including the option to post your resume for viewing and critique by other Vault.com members before you send it out to employers.

Yahoo! HotJobs—http://hotjobs.yahoo.com/. Yahoo! HotJobs lets you screen out jobs posted by staffing firms if you want to deal directly with employers rather than applying through agencies. Search listings by category, company, location, or keyword, or use the advanced search for more options. You can create a Yahoo! HotJobs account to post your resume, set privacy options for your information, and even see statistics on how often your resume is viewed by employers. Yahoo! HotJobs also features job search agents that e-mail you openings matching your criteria and allows you to apply online.

*Special thanks to **Kirsten Dixson** of Brandego (www.brandego.com) for lending her cutting-edge resume and technology expertise to the update of this chapter for the second edition of this book. Kirsten is a true pioneer in leveraging technology to help people increase their career success. She is a Founding Partner of Brandego, where she works with her clients to develop and manage their online identities with branded Web portfolios and blogs, and she is the cofounder of the Reach Branding Club, a virtual coaching environment for personal branding. She also serves as the Technology Master for the Career Masters Institute.*

Chapter 6

Write a Better Resume Now

After completing some or all of chapters 1 and 2, you are ready to put together a "better" resume. By better, I mean one that is more carefully crafted than those you have already done. This chapter will help you pull together what you have learned and create an effective resume. It also expands on tips in chapter 2 on how to design, produce, and use your resume to best effect.

This chapter assumes that you have read and done the activities in chapters 1, 2, and 3. I also assume that you have done a basic resume as outlined in those chapters, and I hope you have taken my advice to use it right away while you worked on creating a "better" resume as time permitted.

If You Aren't Good at This, Get Some Help

If you are not particularly good at writing and designing a resume, consider getting help with various elements. Several sources of help are available.

Professional Resume Writers

The fees that some resume writers charge are a bargain, while others charge entirely too much for what you get. And an inexpensive resume might not be a bargain if it is done poorly. Few regulations or requirements exist for setting up business as a resume writer, and the quality and pricing of services vary widely.

In reviewing a resume writer's capabilities, you need to have a good idea of the services you want and buy only those you need. For example, some resume writers have substantial experience and skills in career counseling and can help you clarify what you want to do. Helping you write your resume might be the end result of more expensive, time-consuming career counseling services that you might or might not need. Most professional resume writers ask you questions about your skills, experiences, and accomplishments so that they can use this information to improve your resume. This expertise will benefit almost everyone.

But, in some cases, the writer is essentially a keyboarder who takes the information you provide and puts it into a simple format without asking questions. This service does not have the same value and obviously should cost less.

Some resume writers provide additional services. These services include printing a number of resumes and envelopes, putting your resume on a computer disc or e-mailing it to you as an attachment (for future changes you can make), putting your resume into an electronic format for Internet posting, or posting your electronic resume on one or more Internet sites.

> **TIP:** *You can locate resume writers through the yellow pages under "Resume Service" or similar headings. Also, you can often find their ads in the newspaper's help-wanted section. You can also find them through professional organizations (see the sidebar later in this chapter). But perhaps the best source is through a referral by someone who has used a specific writer, so ask around.*

I said early in this book that writing a good resume creates structure that will help you clarify what you want to do in a career sense. That process is not simple, and you might benefit greatly from the help of a true career-counseling professional who also happens to be a resume writer. On the other hand, you can also get ripped off, so ask for prices and know exactly what is included before you commit to any resume-writing services.

Ask for Credentials

Four major associations of professional resume writers exist—the Professional Association of Résumé Writers and Career Coaches (PARW/CC; www.parw.com), the National Résumé Writers' Association (NRWA; www.nrwa.com), Career Directors International (CDI; www.careerdirectors.com), and the Career Masters Institute (CMI; www.cminstitute.com). These affiliations are often included in yellow pages advertisements. Because each of these associations has a code of ethics, someone who belongs to one or more of these groups offers better assurance of legitimate services.

Better yet is someone who is a Certified Professional Resume Writer (CPRW), Nationally Certified Resume Writer (NCRW), Certified Resume Writer (CARW, CERW, or CMRW), Master Resume Writer (MRW), or similar designation, a process that requires passing resume-writing competency tests. In any situation, ask for the credentials of the person who will provide the service and see examples of the person's work before you agree to anything.

Members of these associations wrote many of the sample resumes in chapter 7. As you can see, those writers are very good at what they do.

Career or Job Search Counselors and Counseling Services

In your search for someone to help you with your resume, you might run into high-pressure efforts to sell you services. If so, buyer beware! Good, legitimate job search and career professionals are out there, and they are worth every bit of their reasonable fees. Many employers pay thousands of dollars for outplacement assistance to help those leaving find new jobs. But some career-counseling businesses prey on unsuspecting, vulnerable souls who are unemployed. Some "packages" can cost thousands of dollars and are not worth the price.

I have said for years that many job seekers would gain more from reading a few good job search books than they might get from the less-than-legitimate businesses offering these services. But how do you tell the legitimate from the illegitimate? One clue is high-pressure sales and high fees. If this is the case, your best bet is to walk out quickly. Call the agency first and get some information on services offered and prices charged. If the agency requires that you come in to discuss this, assume that it is a high-pressure sales outfit and avoid it.

TIP: *Low-cost services often are available from local colleges or other organizations. These may consist of workshops and access to reading materials, assessment tests, and other services at a modest or even no cost. Consider these as an alternative to higher-priced services, and be sure to compare and contrast what you're getting.*

Improve Your Chronological Resume

You learned to create a basic chronological resume in chapter 2. Although a traditional chronological resume has limitations, you can add some information and modify its style to your advantage. Here are some things you can do, depending on your situation.

Add a Job Objective

Although a chronological resume might not include a job objective, yours certainly can. Although this limits your candidacy to certain types of jobs, you should be focusing your job search in this way for other reasons. And including a job objective allows you to focus your resume content to best support that objective.

Emphasize Skills and Accomplishments

Most chronological resumes simply provide a listing of tasks, duties, and responsibilities. But if you have included a job objective, you should clearly emphasize skills, accomplishments, and results that support that objective.

Expand Your Education and Training Section

Let's say that you are a recent graduate who worked your way through school, earned decent grades (while working full time), and got involved in extracurricular activities. The standard listing of education would not do you justice, so consider expanding that section to include statements about your accomplishments while going to school.

Add New Sections to Highlight Your Strengths

There is no reason you can't add one or more sections to your resume to highlight something you think will help you. For example, let's say you have excellent references from previous employers. You might add a statement to that effect and even include one or more positive quotes. Or maybe you got exceptional performance reviews, wrote some articles, edited a newsletter, traveled extensively, or did something else that might support your job objective. If so, nothing prevents you from creating a special section or heading to highlight these activities.

Portfolios and Enclosures

Some occupations typically require a portfolio of your work or some other concrete example of what you have done. Artists, copy writers, advertising people, clothing designers, architects, radio and TV personalities, and many others know this and should take care to provide good examples of what they do.

Examples can include writing samples, photographs of your work, articles you have written, sample audio or videotapes, artwork, and so on. See chapter 5 for more on developing an online version of your portfolio.

Gather Information and Emphasize Accomplishments, Skills, and Results

Chapter 2 included a worksheet designed to gather essential information for your resume. This chapter includes an expanded worksheet to help you gather the information that is most important to include in a resume. Some information is the same as that called for in the Instant Resume Worksheet in chapter 2, but this new worksheet is considerably more thorough. If you complete it carefully, it will prepare you for the final step of writing a superior resume.

COMPREHENSIVE RESUME WORKSHEET

Use this worksheet to write a draft of the material you will include in your resume. Use a writing style similar to that of your resume, emphasizing skills and accomplishments. Keep your narrative as brief as possible and make every word count.

Use a pencil or erasable pen to allow for changes. You might find it helpful to use a separate sheet of paper for drafting the information for some worksheet sections. After you do that, go ahead and complete the worksheet in the book. The information you write on the worksheet should be pretty close to the information you will use to write your resume, so write it carefully.

(continued)

(continued)

Personal Identification

Name

Home address

City, state or province, ZIP or postal code

Primary phone number

Comment

Alternate/cell phone number

Comment

E-mail address

Job Objective Statement

Write your job objective here, as you would like it to appear on your resume. Writing a good job objective is tricky business and requires a good sense of what you want to do as well as the skills you have to offer. You might want to review sample resumes in chapter 7 before completing this.

In Just a Few Words, Why Should Someone Hire You?

A good resume will answer this question in some way. So, to clarify the essential reasons why someone should hire you over others, write a brief answer to the question in the following space. Then, in some way, make sure that your resume gets this across.

_____

_____

_____

_____

Key Adaptive Skills to Emphasize in Your Resume

Adaptive skills are skills you use every day to survive and get along, such as getting to work on time, honesty, enthusiasm, and getting along with others. What key adaptive skills do you have that support your stated job objective? List the skills that best support your job objective. After each, write the accomplishments or experiences that best support those skills—proof that you have these skills. Be brief and emphasize numbers and results when possible. Include some or all of these skills in your resume.

Adaptive skill _____

Proof of this skill _____

_____

_____

_____

_____

Adaptive skill _____

Proof of this skill _____

_____

_____

_____

_____

Adaptive skill _____

(continued)

(continued)

Proof of this skill _____

_____

_____

_____

_____

Key Transferable Skills to Emphasize in Your Resume

Transferable skills are general skills that can be useful in a variety of jobs, such as writing clearly, good language skills, and the ability to organize and prioritize tasks. Select your transferable skills that best support your stated job objective. List them, along with examples of when you used or demonstrated these skills. Use some or all of these in your resume.

Transferable skill _____

Proof of this skill _____

_____

_____

_____

Transferable skill _____

Proof of this skill _____

_____

_____

_____

Transferable skill _____

Proof of this skill _____

_____

Transferable skill

Proof of this skill

Transferable skill

Proof of this skill

What Are the Key Job Related Skills Needed in the Job You Want?

Job-related skills are those needed to perform a particular job or type of job, such as repairing brakes or using a computer accounting program. If you have selected an appropriate job objective, you should have the exact skills needed for that job. Write the most important job-related skills (more if you know them), along with examples to support these skills—and include them in your resume.

Job-related skill

Proof of this skill

(continued)

(continued)

Job-related skill

Proof of this skill

Job-related skill

Proof of this skill

Job-related skill

Proof of this skill

Job-related skill

Proof of this skill

What Specific Work or Other Experience Do You Have That Supports Your Doing This Job?

If you are doing a chronological resume, you should organize the information in order of the jobs you have held. If you are doing a skills resume, organize the information within major skill areas. I suggest you complete both sections. In doing so, write the content as if you were writing it for use on your resume. You can, of course, further edit what you write here into its final form, but try to approximate the writing style you will use in your resume. Use short sentences. Include action words. Emphasize key skills. Include numbers to support your skills and emphasize accomplishments and results instead of simply listing your duties.

In previous jobs that don't relate well to what you want to do next, emphasize adaptive and transferable skills and accomplishments that relate to the job you want. Mention promotions, raises, or positive evaluations as appropriate. If you did more than your job title suggests, consider a title that is more descriptive (but not misleading) such as "head waiter and assistant manager," if that is what you were, instead of "waiter." If you had a number of short-term jobs, consider combining them all under one heading such as "Various Jobs While Attending College."

You might need to complete several drafts of this information before it begins to "feel good," so use additional sheets of paper as needed.

Experiences Organized by Chronology

Most recent or present job title_____

Dates (month/year) from_____to_____

Organization name_____

City, state or province, ZIP or postal code_____

_____

Duties, skills, responsibilities, accomplishments_____

(continued)

(continued)

Next most recent job title

Dates (month/year) from _____ to _____

Organization name

City, state or province, ZIP or postal code

Duties, skills, responsibilities, accomplishments

Next most recent job title

Dates (month/year) from _____ to _____

Organization name

City, state or province, ZIP or postal code

Duties, skills, responsibilities, accomplishments

Next most recent job title _____

Dates (month/year) from _____ to _____

Organization name _____

City, state or province, ZIP or postal code _____

Duties, skills, responsibilities, accomplishments _____

_____

_____

_____

_____

Experience Organized by Skills

Skills resumes often include statements regarding accomplishments and results as well as duties. They also often mention other skills that are related to or support the key skill as well as specific examples. These can be work-related experiences or can come from other life experiences.

Assume for now that your resume will organize your experience under key skills. Begin by listing the three to six skills you consider to be most important to succeed in the job you want. When you decide which ones to list, write in examples of experiences and accomplishments that directly support these skills. Write this just as you want it to appear in your resume.

Key skill 1 _____

Resume statement to support this skill _____

_____

_____

(continued)

(continued)

_____

_____

Key skill 2 _____

Resume statement to support this skill _____

_____

_____

_____

Key skill 3 _____

Resume statement to support this skill _____

_____

_____

_____

Key skill 4 _____

Resume statement to support this skill _____

_____

_____

_____

Key skill 5 _____

Resume statement to support this skill _____

_____

_____

_____

Key skill 6

Resume statement to support this skill

What Education or Training Supports Your Job Objective?

In writing your education and training section, be sure to include any additional information that supports your qualifications for your job objective. New graduates should emphasize their education and training more than experienced workers and include more details in this section.

Use the space that follows to write what you want to include on your resume under the education and training heading.

School or training institution attended

Dates attended or graduated

Degree or certification obtained

Anything else that should be mentioned

School or training institution attended

Dates attended or graduated

Degree or certification obtained

Anything else that should be mentioned

(continued)

(continued)

School or training institution attended

Dates attended or graduated

Degree or certification obtained

Anything else that should be mentioned

Other Formal or Informal Training That Supports Your Job Objective

Other Resume Sections

If you want to include other sections on your resume, write their headings and whatever you want to include. Examples might be "Summary of Experience," "Special Accomplishments," or others. See the headings of this kind among the sample resumes in chapter 7 for inspiration.

More Quick Resume-Writing Tips

Chapters 1 through 3 covered the basics of writing a resume, but here are some additional tips and information you might find helpful.

As Much as Possible, Write Your Resume Yourself

I have come to realize that some people, even very smart people who are good writers, can't write or design a good resume. And there is no good reason to force them to write one from start to finish. If you are one of these people, just decide that your skills are in other areas and don't go looking for a job as a resume writer. Get someone else, preferably a professional resume writer, to do it for you.

But even if you don't write your own resume, you should do as much as possible yourself. The reason is that, if you don't, your resume won't be truly yours. Your resume might present you well, but it won't be *you*. Not only might your resume misrepresent you to at least some extent, you also will not have learned what you need to learn by going through the process of writing your resume. You would not have struggled with your job objective statement in the same way and might not have as clear a sense of what you want to do as a result. You would not have the same understanding of the skills you have to support your job objective. As a result, you probably won't do as well in an interview.

So, even though I encourage you to "borrow" ideas from this book's sample resumes, your resume must end up being yours. You have to be able to defend its content and prove each and every statement you've made. Even if you end up hiring someone to help with your resume, you must provide this person with what to say and let him or her help you with how to say it. If you don't agree with something the writer does, ask the person to change it to your specifications. However you do it, make sure that your resume is *your* resume and that it represents you accurately.

Don't Lie or Exaggerate

Some job applicants misrepresent themselves. They lie about where they went to school or say that they have a degree that they do not have. They state previous salaries that are higher than they really were. They present themselves as having responsibilities and titles that are not close to the truth.

I do not recommend you do this. For one reason, it is simply not right, and that is reason enough. But there are also practical reasons for not doing so. The first is that you might get a job that you can't handle. If that were to happen, and you fail, it would serve you right. Another reason is that some employers check references and backgrounds more thoroughly than you might realize. Sometimes, this can occur years after you are employed and, if you are caught, you could lose your job, which would not be a pleasant experience.

So, my advice is this: Honesty is the best policy.

Never Include a Negative

Telling the truth does not mean you have to tell *everything*. Some things are better left unsaid, and a resume should present your strengths and not your weaknesses. In writing your resume, you should *never* include anything employers might interpret as a negative. For example, if you are competing with people who have a degree and you don't, it is better to not mention your education (or, in this case, lack of it). Instead, emphasize your skills and accomplishments. If you can do the job, it really shouldn't matter, and many employers will hire based on what you can do, rather than on what you don't have.

Trust me on this: If you can honestly and convincingly tell employers why they should hire you over someone else, they probably will.

This Is No Place to Be Humble

Being honest on your resume does not mean you can't present the facts in the most positive way. A resume is not a place to be humble. So work on *what* you say and *how* you say it, so that you present your experiences and skills as positively as possible.

Use Short Sentences and Simple Words

Short sentences are easier to read. They communicate better than long ones. Simple words also communicate more clearly than long ones. So use short sentences and easy-to-understand words in your resume (like I've done in this paragraph).

Many people like to throw in words and phrases that are related to their field but are not used elsewhere. Some of this might be necessary, but too often I see language that is too specialized, which will turn off many employers. Good writing is easy to read and understand. It is harder to do but is worth the time.

If It Doesn't Support Your Job Objective, Cut It Out

A resume is only one or two pages long, so you have to be careful what you do and do not include. Review each and every word and ask yourself, "Does this support my ability to do the job in some clear way?" If that item does not support your job objective, it should go.

Include Numbers

Many sample resumes in chapter 7 include some numbers. They could refer to the speed at which someone does word processing, the number of transactions processed per month, the percentage of increased sales, the number of people or orders processed, or some other numerical measure of performance. Numbers communicate in a special way, and you should include numbers to support key skills you have or that reflect your accomplishments or results.

Emphasize Skills

It should be obvious by now that you should emphasize skills in your resume. Besides listing the key skills needed to support your job objective in a skills resume, you should include a variety of skill statements in all narrative sections of your resume. In each case, select skills you have that support your job objective.

Highlight Accomplishments and Results

Anyone can go through the motions of doing a job, but employers want to know how well you have done things in the past. Did you accomplish anything out of the ordinary? What results did you achieve?

The Importance of Doing Drafts

It will probably take you several rewrites before you are satisfied with your resume's content. And it will take even more changes before you are finished. Writing, modifying, editing, changing, adding to, and subtracting from content are important steps in writing a good resume. For this reason, I suggest that you write yours on a computer if you can, so that you can make changes quickly.

Edit, Edit, Edit

Every word has to count in your resume, so keep editing until it is right. This might require you to make multiple passes and to change your resume many times. But, if you did as I suggested and have created a simple but acceptable resume, fretting over your "better" resume shouldn't delay your job search one bit. Right?

Get Someone Else to Review Your Resume for Errors

After you have finished writing your resume, ask someone with good spelling and grammar skills to review it once again. It is simply amazing how efforts crepe into the most carefully edit resume (like the ones in this very sentence).

More Tips to Improve Your Resume's Design and Appearance

Just as some people aren't good at resume writing, others are not good at design. Many resumes use simple designs, and this is acceptable for most situations. But you can do other things to improve your resume's appearance.

Increase Readability with Some Simple Design Principles

People who design advertising know what makes something easy or hard to read—and they work very hard to make things easy. Here are some things they have found to improve readability. You can apply these same principles in writing your resume.

> **TIP:** When looking at the sample resumes in chapter 7, note how some have a better appearance than others. Some have rules and bullets; others do not. Some include more white space whereas others are quite crowded. Compromises are made in most resumes, but some clearly look better than others. Note the resumes with the appearances you like and try to incorporate those design principles in your own resume.

- Short sentences and short words are better than long ones.

- Short paragraphs are easier to read than long ones.

- Narrow columns are easier to read than wide ones.

- Put important information on the top and to the left because people scan materials from left to right and top to bottom.

- Using plenty of white space increases the text's readability. And it looks better.

- Don't use too many type styles (fonts) on the same page. Using one or two fonts is ideal; three is pushing it.

- Use underlining, bold type, and bullets to emphasize and separate—but use them sparingly.

Avoid "Packing" Your Resume with Small Print

Sometimes it's hard to avoid including lots of detail, but doing so can make your resume appear crowded and hard to read. In many cases, you can shorten a crowded resume with good editing, which would allow for considerably more white space.

Use Two Pages at the Most

One page is often enough if you are disciplined in your editing, but two uncrowded pages are far better than one crowded one. Those with considerable experience or high levels of responsibility often require a two-page resume, but very, very few justify more than two. (An exception would be the resume for an editor on pages 155–157, which uses a third page as an addendum listing published writing work.)

> **TIP:** *If you end up with one and a half pages of resume, add content or white space until it fills the whole two pages. It just looks better.*

Use Type Fonts Sparingly

Just because you have many type fonts on your computer does not mean you have to use them all on your resume. Doing so creates a cluttered, hard-to-read look and is a sure sign of someone without design skills. Good resume design requires relatively few and easy-to-read fonts in limited sizes. Look at the sample resumes in chapter 7—few use more than one or two type fonts. They also use bold and different-sized fonts sparingly.

Consider Graphics

I included some sample resumes in chapter 7 that use graphic elements to make them more interesting. Although resumes with extensive graphic design elements are not the focus for this book, some resumes clearly benefit from this. Good graphic design is more important for those in creative jobs such as advertising, art, and desktop publishing. One book that emphasizes resumes with great graphic designs, papers, shapes, and other features is *The Edge Resume and Job Search Strategy* by Bill Corbin and Shelbi Wright (JIST Publishing).

Edit Again for Appearance

Just as your resume's text requires editing, you should be prepared to review and make additional changes to your resume's design. After you have written the content just as you want it, you will probably need to make additional editing and design changes so that everything looks right.

Select Top-Quality Paper

Don't use cheap copy-machine paper. After all your work, you should use only top-quality paper. Most print shops are used to doing resumes and will have appropriate paper selections. The better-quality papers often contain a percentage of cotton or other fibers. I prefer an off-white or light cream color because it gives a professional, clean appearance.

Envelopes made of the same paper as your resume present a professional look. Select an envelope of the same paper type and color at the time you choose your resume paper. You should also get some blank sheets of this same paper for your cover letters and other job search correspondence. In some cases, you might also be able to obtain matching thank-you note envelopes and paper.

More Tips on Production and Getting Copies Made

Here are a few resume production tips.

Good-Quality Photocopies and Laser Printer Copies Are Fine

Many photocopy machines now create excellent images, and you can use these to reproduce your resume—as long as you use high-grade paper. Test the copy quality first. Most laser printers also create good-quality images; you can use them to make multiple copies of your resume.

> **TIP:** If someone else will help you with the design of your resume, bring this person copies of resumes you like as design examples. Be open to suggestions, but be willing to assert your taste regarding your resume's final appearance.

Evaluating and Selecting a Quick Print Shop

Because of the quality you can get from good photocopiers and laser printers, I don't think it is necessary to use an offset printer. If you take your photocopying to a quick-print shop, however, ask to see examples first.

There are many quick-print shops in the yellow pages under "Printers." Look for a smaller shop that specializes in small jobs rather than a commercial printer that prints hundreds or thousands of copies at once.

How Many Copies to Get

If you will print your resume on your own laser or ink-jet printer, print enough to have extras on hand at all times. You just never know when you might need to give one out. If you are photocopying your resume, get at least 50 copies.

The best use of your resume is to get it into circulation early and often—have enough so that you don't feel like you need to "save" them. Plan on giving multiple copies to friends, relatives, and acquaintances and sending out lots prior to and after interviews.

Chapter 7

A Stupendous Collection of Professionally Written and Designed Resumes

The resumes in this section were written by professional resume writers. As a result, they present a wonderful variety of writing and design styles and techniques. Each was written with great care and skill to present a real (but fictionalized) person in the best way possible. This approach is much more helpful than showing you lots of resumes by the same writer, using the same format.

I want to thank the writers who submitted resumes, all of them members of the Career Masters Institute (www.cminstitute.com). There were so many good ones that I could have done a 1,000-page book!

How to Use the Sample Resumes in This Section

I've never felt that there was one right way to do a resume. Each person has unique information to present, and each resume can look and be different. Often there are good reasons for this. For example, some occupations (such as accounting or law) have more formal traditions, so those resumes typically are more formal. Someone looking for a job in graphic design or marketing might have a more colorful, graphic, and nontraditional resume.

There are many reasons to use different writing and design styles, and the resumes in this section show wide variety in all their elements. There are samples of chronological, skills, combination, and creative resumes. There are resumes for all sorts of people looking for all sorts of jobs. Some resumes include interesting graphic elements and others are quite plain.

This variety will give you ideas for writing and creating your own resume. Feel free to experiment and use whatever style best suits you.

Resumes for All Types of Jobs

I have organized the resumes into groups that should be helpful to you:

- Health care...pages 122–127.
- Computers... pages 128–131.
- Technical... pages 132–135.
- Education and training... pages 136–140.
- Management... pages 141–144.
- Executives... pages 145–147.
- Sales and marketing... pages 148–153.
- Creative and media... pages 154–157.
- Clerical... pages 158–162.
- Accounting... pages 163–164.
- Trades... pages 165–168.
- Service... pages 169–172.
- Career changers... pages 173–176.
- New graduates... pages 177–180.
- Still in school... pages 181–182.
- No degree/no college... pages 183–186.
- Military-to-civilian transitions... pages 187–189.
- Entrepreneur... page 190.

One obvious way to use the samples is to turn to the section that seems most compatible with your career goals. You can see how others in similar situations or seeking similar jobs have handled their resumes. But I also encourage you to look at all the samples for formats, presentation styles, and other ideas to use in your resume. For example, some resumes have superior graphic design elements that might inspire you, even though your job objective lies in a different area.

The comments on the resumes point out features, provide information about the person behind the resume, or give other details. They give you insights into the professional resume writers' thoughts and strategies for presenting these candidates in the best possible light.

A simple functional format

DIAMOND LIPTON
CERTIFIED NURSING ASSISTANT (CNA)

301-444-1234
dtcna@hotmail.com
5253 Hammond Ct.
Bowie, Maryland 20718

HIGHLIGHTS OF QUALIFICATIONS

Recent certification is highlighted

- Completed CNA Certificate Program, 2005.
- Skilled CNA with three years of experience, successfully performing routine tasks under supervision of nursing staff.
- Provided administrative and secretarial support to technical services staff.
- Excellent communication skills, friendly and dependable.

PROFESSIONAL SKILLS

Skills are emphasized here

Patient Care Skills
- Provide patient care such as bathing, dressing, toileting, and feeding.
- Competent in collecting, measuring, and recording liquid output.
- Assist in care of patient with external or internal urinary catheters; nasogastric tubes; intravenous tubes; and oxygen therapy.
- Skilled in application of nonsterile dry dressings and bandages.

Vital Signs and Emergency Procedures
- Skilled at recording temperature, pulse, and respiration using various methods.
- Able to pinpoint and recognize signs and symptoms of distress and provide immediate temporary intervention.

Rehabilitative and Ambulatory Skills
- Assist in ambulating, using rules of body mechanics.
- Transfer and turn patients for comfort and safety.
- Assist in preventing the physical complications of inactivity.
- Promote individual activities using tools and techniques for healthy daily living.

RELEVANT WORK EXPERIENCE

01/04–03/05 Erickson Retirement Communities, Silver Springs, MD
02/04–09/04 Fairhaven Assisted Living, Sykesville, MD

EDUCATION AND TRAINING

2005 Certified Nursing Assistant Training
Regional Occupational Program, Baltimore, MD

Submitted by Brenda Thompson

ERICA CLAYTON

2625 Trancas St. • Napa, California 94558 • (707) 257-1183 • eclayton@email.com

DENTAL ASSISTANT
Knowledgeable...Experienced...Professional

PROFILE

Graduate Dental Assistant with chairside, scheduling, reception, and telephone experience in general and endodontic practices. X-ray certified. Experienced in composite and amalgam fillings, oral surgery, root canals, impressions, molds, and crown preparation.

Communicates candidate's enthusiasm

- Tactful, patient and courteous.
- Positive and enthusiastic.
- Professional telephone etiquette.
- Work well independently or as a team member.
- Punctual and responsible with a strong work ethic.

EMPLOYMENT

William Mahoney, D.D.S., Napa, CA
General Practice   11/04–present

Treatment & Case Coordinator, Chairside Assistant
- Manage appointment schedules for three dentists to maximize available treatment time.
- Interface with doctors to implement course of treatment and with patients to arrange payment schedules and appointments.
- Coordinate with labs, suppliers, and office staff to ensure that all elements are in place to meet patients' treatment needs upon arrival for appointment, for example, x rays, impressions, prostheses, etc.
- Maintain supplies inventory to ensure consistent availability of all products.
- Provide patient education and encouragement.
- Assist dentists during treatment.
- Apply fluoride and sealant.

Highlights chairside experience

Samuel Rutherford, D.D.S. & Dr. Roger Ingram, D.D.S.
Napa, CA
Endodontia   1/02–10/04

Chairside Assistant & Front Office
- Assisted in all aspects of treatment and in preparation for treatment, including sterilizing instruments, setting up trays, preparing injections, taking impressions, and pouring molds.
- Educated patients on dental hygiene and post-op care.
- Maintained inventory and ordered supplies.
- Assisted front office with reception, scheduling, filing, and telephones.

Important formal training is listed here

Part-time Positions (student)   10/00–7/02

Hollywood Video	Glendale, CA	Assistant Manager & Trainer
Auntie Mary's Pretzel Palace	Northridge, CA	Shift Manager/Trainer
Runners, Inc.	Simi Valley, CA	Office Assistant

EDUCATION   Certificate in Dental Assisting, ROP, Glendale, CA   6/02

VOLUNTEER   Girl Scouts of America, Glendale, CA (summers)   8/89–8/94
- Designed, coordinated, and implemented fun-filled week-long programs for younger scouts.

COMPUTER SKILLS   Basic knowledge of MS Word and Excel, Internet, and e-mail.

Submitted by Gay Anne Himebaugh

PAULINE E. SWINDELL, RN

333 Hidden Lane
Jackman, MO 00000

pswindell55@aol.com
Cell: (000) 000–0000

◆ EDUCATION ◆

Education is placed at the top because she is a fairly recent graduate

Jackman City College of Nursing, Jackman, MO
Bachelor of Science Degree in **Nursing,** May 2006
☐ Dean's List, three semesters
☐ GPA: 3.65/4.0, with honors

Lafayette Community College, Lafayette, MO
Associate Degree in **Psychology,** May 1998

◆ CLINICAL EXPERIENCE ◆

Heavy black lettering against lots of white space makes the resume appear clean, simple, and straightforward

Spring 2006	**Bensen Hills Hospital,** Jackman, MO *Psychiatric Unit* ▪ Daily interacted with broad range of inpatient psychiatric clients to complete assessments and patient care planning.
Fall 2005	**Jackman City Hospital,** Jackman, MO *Med-surg Post-surgical Unit* ▪ Changed dressings, administered meds and IVs, and removed catheters. ▪ Assisted with insertion of various drains used post-surgically. ▪ Carefully assessed patient inputs and outputs. ▪ Performed EKGs as ordered.
Spring 2005	**Phillip Rheims General Hospital,** Bolton, MO *Maternity* ▪ Trained new parents with proper care of newborns. ▪ Performed postpartum assessments. ▪ Assisted nurses during newborn assessments and birthing procedures. ▪ Evaluated and observed diagnostic procedures during labor and delivery.
Fall 2004	**Saint Theresa Hospital,** Plainville, MO *Pediatric Unit* ▪ Administered all medications as prescribed. ▪ Interacted with children during diversionary activities.
Spring 2004	**Saint Theresa Hospital,** Plainville, MO *Medications and IV Therapy* ▪ Prepared care plans and medications prior to administration. ▪ Completed physical assessments on all patients.

(continues)

Submitted by Edward Turilli

Pauline E. Swindell   Cell: (000) 000-0000
Page Two

Fall 2003   **James L. Betts Retirement Home,** Jackman, MO
                 PTs with ADLs
                 ▪ Intermingled with PTs during group meals.
                 ▪ Administered medications to PTs as required.

Diamond motif helps candidate establish a unique brand identity

◇ RELATED EMPLOYMENT ◇

Jan 2004–   **Jackman City Hospital,** Jackman, MO
Present   *Mental Health Worker,* Part-time
                 ▪ Assess and complete BIWA withdrawal assessment sheets.
                 ▪ Interview PTs to wrap up daily process notes.
                 ▪ Complete observation sheets with appropriate levels of
                   observation for each patient.
                 ▪ Always maintain safe milieu appropriate for patient safety.
                 ▪ Provide crisis intervention as needed.
                 ▪ Readily interact with peers and colleagues in a positive,
                   professional, and therapeutic environment.

Aug 2002–   **Lafayette Child and Family Services,** Lafayette, MO
Jan 2004   *Residential Counselor,* Part-time
                 ▪ Supervised residents' activities, recording daily personnel
                   accountability.
                 ▪ Administered prescription medication as prescribed.
                 ▪ Daily interacted with peers to ensure safe and enjoyable
                   environment.

◇ OTHER EMPLOMENT ◇

Summers   **Lafayette Summer Recreation Center,** Lafayette, MO
2000–2002   *Lifeguard, Swim & Safety Instructor*

◇ CERTIFICATIONS / SKILLS ◇

• Registered Nurse   • Health Care Provider
• CPR, First Aid   • American Red Cross
• Lifeguard   • Crisis Intervention

◇ VOLUNTEER ◇

• First Aid and Safety Member, U.S. Lifeguard Association
• Sylvan-Snyder Children's Care Center: Outpatient Services
• Jackman Youth Intervention Association

MARK FRIEDMAN

23 Plainview Road • Plainview, New York 11590 • (516) 273-9981
markfriedman@optonline.net

Uses a two-column format to make headings easy to find

PROFILE	Physical Therapist who is able to work toward the restoration of function and the elimination of disability in individuals of all ages disabled by illness or an accident, or born with a handicap. Demonstrated skills working in hospitals and rehabilitation centers. Assist industry professionals in planning and directing patient care and preventative programs. Strongly motivated and dedicated to working with patients toward physical independence.
EDUCATION	Touro College • Bay Shore, NY **Bachelor of Science in Health Sciences,** 9/06 **Master of Science in Physical Therapy,** 9/06 Long Island University at C.W. Post Campus • Brookville, NY **Bachelor of Science in Physical Education Non-School,** 5/02 Concentration: Exercise Rehabilitation
CLINICAL ROTATIONS 6/06 to 8/06 Level IV	STONY BROOK UNIVERSITY HOSPITAL • Stony Brook, NY **Acute Care** ~ Treated TKR, THR, CVA, and COPD diagnoses. ~ Provide D/C planning, evaluations, and exercise programs. ~ Associated with multiple disciplines in social work, nursing, and physician care. ~ Observed surgery: Hemiarthroplasty. ~ Participated in rounds and meetings. ~ Assisted Physical Therapists with patient care, exercise programs, and patient/family education. ~ Presented an in-service on Constraint Induced Movement Therapy.
1/06 to 3/06 Level III	PLAINVIEW PHYSICAL THERAPY • Plainview, NY **Outpatient Orthopedic** ~ Evaluated, treated, and discharged patients with TKR, THR, ACL reconstruction, RC tear, shoulder impingement syndrome, sports/work-related injuries, LBP, and spinal orthopedic dysfunction; received experience in manual therapy. ~ Chronicled treatments in patients' charts; completed insurance forms. ~ Observed surgery: total knee replacement. ~ Presented an in-service on Total Knee Replacement.

Submitted by Donna Farrise

MARK FRIEDMAN
- Page Two -

4/05 to 6/05 **Level II**	ST. CATHERINE'S HOSPITAL • Smithtown, NY **Inpatient Geriatric Rehabilitation** ~ Reviewed charts; evaluated, treated, and discharged geriatric patients. ~ Primarily treated patients diagnosed with CVA, TKR, and THR. ~ Treated patients with balance problems and assisted with wound care. ~ Presented a case study on a patient with Parkinson's Disease and Chronic Obstructive Pulmonary Disease. ~ Presented an in-service on "The Effects of Tai Chi on Balance in the Elderly Populations."
10/04 to 12/04 **Level I**	ST. MARY'S HOSPITAL • Brooklyn, NY **Outpatient Physical Therapy** ~ Evaluated, treated, and discharged adults/pediatrics from outpatient physical therapy. ~ Treated MS, CVA, BKA, AKA, patella tendonitis, bicep contractures, and Erb's Palsy diagnoses. ~ Observed wound care of amputated lower extremities.
PROFESSIONAL **EXPERIENCE** **6/00 to 5/03**	ALL CARE PHYSICAL THERAPY & REHABILITATION • Freeport, NY **Outpatient Rehabilitation Physical Therapy Aide** ~ Assisted with patient care, exercise programs, gym supervision, and application of heat, cold, electric stimulation, and ultrasound machines. ~ Educated patients and their families on treatment programs, care, symptoms, and potential complications. *~ Designed a pool therapy packet for patients to be treated through aquatic therapy.*

Relevant experience before getting his degree is included later in the resume

CERTIFICATIONS Adult/Infant CPR & First Aid Certified, American Red Cross

Professional memberships show that the candidate is active in the PT field

PROFESSIONAL **MEMBERSHIPS**	American Physical Therapy Association (APTA) Orthopedic Chapter & Sports Physical Therapy Section Member
VOLUNTEER	Empire State Games, Garden City, NY **(25 Hours)** Nassau County Medical Center, East Meadow, NY - Outpatient Physical Therapy Department **(29 hours)**

JAMES CARRO

408 Springmeadow • Holbrook, New York 11741 • (631) 567-9183
jcarro@aol.com

Profile section summarizes the candidate's skills

PROFILE

Helpdesk/Desktop Support Specialist able to provide theoretical and practical customer/user service and support to diagnose, troubleshoot, and repair hardware, software, and peripheral problems. Skilled in applying analytical and technical skills to produce practical solutions. Experienced in the installation of state-of-the-art hardware and software applications. Knowledge of equipment bases, digital switches, hubs, patch cables, routers, servers, administrator stations, network closet wiring, and installation procedures.

TECHNICAL EDUCATION

Install, Upgrade, Migrate & Configure

Details of technical training

Hardware: Pentium 4/D, Celeron
Language: HTML 4.01
Operating Systems: Windows XP/Server 2003
Software: MS Word/Office/Outlook/Access ■ Lotus Notes ■ Netscape Internet Explorer ■ Norton Utilities
Communications: Protocol/SCSI/IDE/MFM/RLL/ESDI ■ **Interface**/Modems/Network Cards/I/O Ports

EDUCATION

Boston University, Boston, MA
**Windows Server 2003/HTML 4.01
Certification (in progress)**
PC Tech & Support Program, **A+ Certification, 2003**

Certifications are included in the Education section

MEDICAL GROUP • Oakdale, NY   **2002 to Present**
Independent Computer Support Contractor
Build computers from board level, install operating systems and software, and configure systems. Perform multiple installations of IE 6 and Fax Sr. from LAN.
~ *Researched components for value and reliability, resulting in substantial savings to customers.*

CERIDIAN PERFORMANCE PARTNERS • Boston, MA   **1999 to 2002**
Fulfillment Coordinator
Performed as visibility liaison among company and human resource departments of subscribing Fortune 500 clients. Ensured timely and cost-efficient fulfillment of material for affiliate and client events. Worked with UPS Online System and Federal Express Powership updating and maintaining affiliate and client database. In conjunction with production department, defined and maintained online inventory system for offsite service facility.

LAURA ASHLEY GLOBAL DEVELOPMENT • Boston, MA   **1996 to 1999**
Mail Services Supervisor
Distributed U.S. and interoffice mail, including payroll, to a staff of 300. Operated and upgraded Pitney Bowes mailing systems. Maintained database of 200 North American shops, U.K. headquarters, and European satellite offices.
~ *Contributed creatively to marketing department's nationwide window-display advertising.*
~ *Trained personnel in applications of UPS Online Shipping and Federal Express PowerShip.*

Submitted by Donna Farrise

William C. Hedges

555 Ridge Road, Princeton, NJ 08540
(609) 921-5555 Work • (609) 921-5566 Fax • billhedges@tgi.com

QUALIFICATIONS

Summary pinpoints career target and highlights technical skills

- ☑ **Database Programmer. Computer Programmer**—applications in C/C++ and Java
- ☑ Proactive team player with proven communications and organization talents.
- ☑ Computer skills: C/C++, STL (Standard Template Library), Java (JDK 1.2), Visual Basic 5, Oracle (SQL, SQL*Plus, PL/SQL), DataEase, Windows 2003, Windows XP, UNIX.

PROFESSIONAL EXPERIENCE

Experience includes class projects

Technical Skills & Programming

- **Point-of-Sales, AR/AP System** for Technology Group, Inc.
  Created a normalized relational database (using DataEase) to provide complete invoicing, billing, and accounts receivable / accounts payable system for $1 million business with 300 active accounts and mailing list of 3,500. Currently running on Windows XP network.

- **Client-Server Sales Module in Java**—Class Project
  Using TCP/IP sockets, connected GUI front end to console application, allowing user to query server for price, availability, and credit status. Provided for simple update functionality.

- **C/C++**—Class Project
  Binary search tree. 2–3 search tree. Quick sort on linked list. String class. STL.

- **Sales Module in Visual Basic Connected to Access Database**—Class Project
  Created GUI front end to Access database (using Visual Basic) allowing input of customer information, part numbers, and quantities; and enabling users to place orders and print invoices and sales summaries.

- **Billing System in Oracle**—Class Project
  Generated users, tables, views, sequences and triggers using SQL, SQL*Plus, and PL/SQL to create Oracle database. Imported data and used Developer 2000 to create forms.

Leadership & Organization Skills

- Spearheaded growth of mail-order business from $50,000 to $700,000 annually. Developed export customers in Europe, Africa, the Middle East, and Australia.

- Provide cross-functional expertise in overseeing daily operations, including technology, accounting, bookkeeping, taxes, purchasing, personnel, marketing, and customer relations.

EDUCATION

Technology Institute of New Jersey, Somerset, NJ—2005 to 2006
Computer Science / Technology Coursework—19 credits, GPA 4.0
Data Structures and Algorithms, C++, Java, Visual Basic, Oracle/SQL, Networking

EMPLOYMENT HISTORY

Employment moved close to the end because it's not as relevant to his career goal

Owner / General Business Manager, Technology Group, Inc., Princeton, NJ—1992 to present
One of the largest beekeeping supply companies on the East Coast

PROFESSIONAL ASSOCIATIONS

Computing Machinery Professionals Association—CMPA
New Jersey CMPA / TECE Joint Chapter
New Jersey Computer Users Group

Submitted by Susan Guarneri

ROBERT M. SCHULTZ

2511 Rangeline Drive, Dallas, Texas 75999 · 452-555-5555 · rmschultz@evansresumes.com

Summary section starts off the resume with skills and areas of experise

SENIOR NETWORK MAINTENANCE / ADVISORY ENGINEER

Customer-focused technical professional with continual recognition for technical proficiency, leadership, and performance exceeding expectations. Characterized as a versatile networking Subject-Matter Expert with demonstrated mastery of broadband and data technologies, as well as ATM, frame relay, Cisco routing, Adtran/Alcatel equipment, and critical NOC engineering standards. *Additional expertise and success in*

- Inventory Management
- Staff Mentoring & Training
- Equipment Staging Approvals
- Project Coordination
- Technical Documentation
- Procedures Standardization
- Customer Requirements
- Shipping & Warehousing
- Equipment Troubleshooting

TECHNICAL BACKGROUND *Certifications and hardware/software are placed in the prime spot on page 1*

Certifications:	TP76300; Level 4 Installer; Cisco 8850/8250, Lucent CBX500, Alcatel/Newbridge 36170/36177/36060/7670, GX 550, and Cascade 9000 Frame Equipment
Hardware:	Adtran TA3000/HDX DSLAM; Alcatel 7300 HD, LP-UD DSLAM, 7470/7670 ATM Switches; Cisco MGX-8850 ATM Switches, 2600 Routers/1900 Switches; Spirent 3577A CopperMax ADSL Test Head; RT DSLAM DC Power Plants
Software:	Microsoft PowerPoint, Word, Excel; Remedy Ticket Systems
Networking:	TCP/IP; ATM; Frame Relay; DSL; ISDN; T-1 Circuits; Network Protocol Analyzers

PROFESSIONAL EXPERIENCE

SUPERIOR TECHNICAL SOLUTIONS, INC. (MBC)   1984–Present

Senior Manager Maintenance Engineer, Richardson, TX, 2005–Present

Selected to fill elite technical advisory role, providing 24×7 network engineering services with oversight of 62 MBC central offices and 13-state area. Serve as Tier 2 support expert and first line of resolution for sophisticated network equipment preparation, testing, and installation. Collaborate with Tier 2 and 3 support groups, regional Subject-Matter Experts, Engineering, telephone companies, and Network Operation/Data Operation Center staff to deliver reliable network functionality. Oversee and monitor staging testing to ensure appropriate supplier performance and consistent service quality. Mentor and train maintenance engineers.

Selected Accomplishments:

- Supported 5,000 customers per switch, with responsibility for switches of up to 450G and $1.4M in value.
- Exceeded or met all Ready for Service dates, working closely with Implementation Engineering, Project Management, vendors, and installation teams.
- Authorized equipment readiness with final word on testing verifications, serving as expert resource instrumental in preserving installation integrity.
- Verified workaround solutions implementation and managed staff coordination to audit fulfillment of high-profile customer requirements.
- Tested Alcatel, Adtran, RPATS, AI/CODCN platforms, and fiber, DDP panel, and FOT panel equipment. Tuned and tested ATM, frame relay, LAN/WAN, Newbridge, TCP/IP, DSL, and Cisco equipment/protocols.

Senior Maintenance Engineer, Richardson, TX, 2003–2005

Served as technical lead charged with 24×7 technical support, new service hardware and software deployment, and maintenance services for data and broadband technologies including ADSL, frame relay, ATM, and routing. Key functions included supporting field engineers in network system diagnostics, on-site technical assistance, and project management for enhancements and installations.

Continued…

Submitted by Laura Smith-Proulx

ROBERT M. SCHULTZ   PAGE TWO

Selected Accomplishments:

- Ensured 100% system availability with timely problem resolution, network problem troubleshooting, and implementation of emergency procedures.
- Worked with regional Subject-Matter Experts to coordinate and implement all new products, FOAs, Engineering Complaints, Maintenance Engineering Flashes, and Product Change Notifications.
- Authored Maintenance Engineering Test & Acceptance procedures for Alcatel 7300 LP-UD DSLAM platform.
- Conducted technical reviews to identify and correct vulnerabilities and deviations from corporate standards.

Maintenance Engineer / Manager Technical Support, Irving, TX, 2001–2003

Promoted to oversee ATM switch installations, as well as preparation for shipping readiness, in close collaboration with Cisco, Alcatel, and Lucent. Served as main regional point of contact. Staged switches according to engineering requests, with full testing to meet industry standards, and inventoried components while maintaining equipment database. Coordinated deliveries with site management, documenting movement and tracking warehouse inventory. Provided monthly hardware failure rate reporting.

Selected Accomplishments:

- Supported department as senior Subject-Matter Expert in Alcatel, Cisco, 7670 Multi-Shelf system, and all computer-related issues.
- Ensured timely replacement of defective equipment, initiating Return Material Authorizations with vendors.
- Supplied Tier 1 technical support to Dallas NOC Transport Technology Center, with TTC ISO 9000 team role critical to turn up, provisioning, maintenance, and upgrade process creation.
- Met 100% of project deadlines, working with diverse array of vendor equipment and keeping Methods of Procedures up-to-date.

System Technician, McKinney, TX, 1984–2001

Installed all special circuits in product line, including OC48 rings, and installed vast array of technologies, including fiber. Detailed crew responsibilities, training and mentoring project technicians. Repaired and implemented DSL equipment on customer premises, and installed and corrected flaws in 911, ARM, OCS, and LAN equipment.

Previous Experience: **System Technician, MAJOR TELEPHONE COMPANY, Dallas, TX**

EDUCATION & PROFESSIONAL DEVELOPMENT

A good strategy for presenting some college, without a degree.

General Studies • RICHLAND COLLEGE, Richardson, TX

Professional Training:

- Fiber Optics
- ATM Newbridge
- CCNA Boot Camp
- Disaster Recovery
- Hazard Recognition
- ISDN Installation & Maintenance
- Data Communications Technology

- SONET Overview
- Digital Synchronization
- Ethics in the Workplace
- Planning and Organizing
- Digital Circuit Technology
- Principles of Digital Transmission
- Network Data Link Lab and Protocols

CIVIC AFFILIATIONS

Certification Candidate and Member, **Community Emergency Response Team (CERT)**

Sherry Gray

107 Pigeon Street ▪ Oakville, Ontario ▪ L5M 2R2
sgray789@hotmail.com

An interesting and relevant graphic draws attention to her technology,
process, and equipment **Mechanical Engineer & Applied Sciences Student**
experience

Technology

- ☑ CAD
- ☑ AutoCAD
- ☑ Maple
- ☑ MATLAB
- ☑ C++
- ☑ G-Code
- ☑ MS Excel

Processes

- ☑ Design Requirements
- ☑ Design Drawings
- ☑ Design Documentation
- ☑ Database Development
- ☑ Quality Assurance

Equipment

- ☑ Coordinates Measuring Machine (CMM)
- ☑ MasterCam
- ☑ Milling Machines
- ☑ Computer Aided Machining (CAM)

Qualifications Summary

Energetic, highly motivated, and organized mechanical engin-eering student with experience in design and development. Well-rounded research and organizational skills along with outstanding communication skills. Personable, independent, and committed to producing top-quality work and results. Positive and upbeat attitude; well liked and respected by peers. Attentive to detail; excellent analytical and problem-solving skills; proven self-starter with strong communication and inter-personal skills. Eager to learn new skills and gain valuable working experience.

Education & Training

University of Ontario, Toronto, Ontario—2003 to present
Bachelor of Engineering and Applied Science

Oakville District High School, Oakville, Ontario—2003
Ontario Secondary School Diploma (O.S.S.D)
- Graduated with Honours

WHIMIS Safety Training—2005

Project and extracurricular experience sets this candidate apart from the competition

Project Experience

- Led, motivated, and organized project team of 3 people in the conceptualization, design, and manufacturing of an electronic monorail system. Resulted in 4th place achievement in competition.

- Added value to students in the faculty and their learning experience through the revitalization of the Executive Committee and membership of the Mechanical Engineer-ing Course Union. Promoted series of inspirational guest speakers that discussed "real-world" job opportunities and requirements for success; redesigned the website to be more informative and interactive; and facilitated meetings on a regular basis.

Volunteer Experience

University of Ontario, Toronto, Ontario—2005
Executive Member, Mechanical Engineering Course Union

The Kinsmen Club of Oakville, Oakville, Ontario—2005
Volunteer

Hospital for Sick Children, Toronto, Ontario—2005
Volunteer

Canadian Cancer Society, Toronto, Ontario—2005
Volunteer

Submitted by Denyse Cowling

PAULA MARTIN
VETERINARY TECHNICIAN
pmartin@protypeltd.com

This candidate landed a job from the very first resume she sent out!

889 Westfield Street
Agawam, MA 06001
413.555.7644

Profile reinforces the diverse clinical and soft skills she offers that relate to her objective

Compassionate and competent **Veterinary Technician** with 6+ years of experience assisting veterinarians in medical and surgical procedures, ranging from routine to emergency and critical care. Recognized as efficient, skilled in multitasking, and dedicated to providing prompt, courteous service. Effective communicator who enjoys working with people and animals and is able to educate owners on protecting their companion animals' health and well-being.

PROFESSIONAL EXPERIENCE

VETERINARY TECHNICIAN
Harrington Animal Clinic, Agawam, MA   *2000 to Present*
Assist 5 veterinarians in providing comprehensive veterinary care. Skilled in performing the following:

Medical & Surgical Procedures
- Assist in all types of medical treatments (and with restraints), ranging from routine office examinations to critical care, emergency situations, euthanasia, and house calls.
- Set up all equipment and prep animals for surgery: shaving, intubating, inserting IV catheters, and administering intravenous/intramuscular drugs.
- Assist with surgeries, including spaying/neutering, exploratory, cystotomy, nasal scope, endoscopy, cruciate/luxating patella, abscess, declawing, and other procedures.
- Prepare and sterilize surgical packs in an autoclave; monitor anesthesia and patients' vital signs. Administer subcutaneous fluids. Perform complete dentistry.
- Accurately document anesthetic drugs used during surgery; handle post-surgical recovery: extubation, patient monitoring, and calling clients to provide follow-up/status reports.
- Prepare vaccines; refill/dispense medications; administer oral medications/vaccines under supervision and provide instructions to clients; assist with administration of chemotherapy.

Tests / Lab Work / Client Education
- Conduct heartworm, Feline Leukemia, and FIV tests. Take glucose and blood (including jugular) samples. Read results of urinalysis and fecal samples.
- Perform and develop radiographs as required. Assist specialists in restraining animals during ultrasounds.
- Educate clients on diseases/preventive care, home care (post surgery, diabetic discharges, and administering subcutaneous fluids and medications), grooming, diet, geriatric care, declawing alternatives, and other aspects of animal health care.
- Groom and bathe animals, including fungal baths, lion clips, and reverse sedation according to veterinarian's instruction.

Experience is organized within skill headings to reinforce the depth of her knowledge and capabilities to work with a wide range of animals

Front Office / Administration
- Cross-trained to perform front office duties, including scheduling routine health exams and surgical appointments, invoicing/cashing out, providing estimates, and more. Greet clients and set up patients in exam rooms.
- Place orders for medications and various products per veterinarians' instructions. Sell products to clients.
- Utilize customized computer applications to process payments and enter patient records.
- Serve as resource to new technicians by answering questions on equipment, office, and other procedures.

EDUCATION / TRAINING

A.S., Veterinary Technician; BRIARWOOD COLLEGE, Springfield, MA   2000

Additional Training:
Completed intensive on-the-job 3-month training under guidance of licensed veterinarians at Harrington Animal Clinic.

Submitted by Louise Garver

An example of a combination format resume

DONALD JACOBS

Confidential Security Clearance

1200 Peninsula Square
Cleveland, Ohio 44122

Home: (216) 333-1234
djacobs01@yahoo.com

A dedicated Electronics Technician with more than ten years of hands-on experience, with the ability to lead and motivate a diverse crew. Experienced in the utilization of creative problem-solving and solution techniques, while exuding decisive and confident decision-making abilities. Skilled in information systems management, with emphasis in program management, and internal control procedures.

Skills are detailed up front

- *Computer Software*—Knowledgeable in MS Word and Excel. Understand C program language and able to perform some software program modifications.
- *Operator Mechanic*—Work closely with engineering personnel to assist in troubleshooting software and hardware using electronic schematics and technical procedures.
- *Quality Assurance*—Write quality reports for non-conformances and repairs conducted.
- *Test Planning*—Plan test environment using required equipment and documentation. Implement test plan with little or no supervision.
- *Troubleshoot and Repair*—Experience with troubleshooting mechanical, electrical, and electronic systems.

Chronological work experience is listed later

EXPERIENCE

AVTRON MANUFACTURING., Independence, OH (2004–Present)
Field Service Engineer
Primary responsibilities include writing service orders, distributing new technical bulletins to the site, training on maintenance practices and scanner operations, coordinating troubleshooting/maintenance with other vendor companies when needed, and assisting technical support group when special testing is being conducted.

COX COMMUNICATIONS, Cleveland, OH (1996–2004)
Operator Mechanic
Responsibilities include daily inspection of all mechanical, electrical, and electronic equipment; chemical analysis of all water systems; performed preventative maintenance and repairs on plant equipment; and wrote work orders for discrepancies.

LINCOLN ELECTRIC, Cleveland, OH (1995–1996)
Mechanical Design Manufacturing Engineer
Responsibilities included designing the in-house manufacturing equipment. Conceptualized equipment and tested the feasibility of the designs. Applied detailed analysis, design, fabrication, installation, debugging techniques, validation, and documentation. Used mechanical engineering theory and practice toward the design of all equipment.

Submitted by Brenda Thompson

Donald Jacobs   Page –2–

UNITED STATES NAVY, Norfolk, VA (1992–1995)
Nuclear Electronics Technician Second Class
Completed more than 4,000 hours of reactor operating time and more than 7,000 hours of logged maintenance and troubleshooting of electronic and microprocessor-based equipment. Duties included repair and maintenance technician, departmental technical librarian, and repair section supervisor of the ship's calibration lab.

EDUCATION

Cleveland State University, Cleveland, OH (1995–2001)
Major: Electrical Engineering
Credits: 64 college semester credits with an overall GPA of 3.68.

NAVY NUCLEAR POWER SCHOOL, Charleston, NC (1991–1992)
- Training consisted of a 24-week course in science and technology designed to provide theoretical background knowledge of nuclear power. It is presumed each officer has successfully completed at least one year of college-level physics and calculus, including integral calculus.

NAVY ELECTRONICS TECHNICIAN SCHOOL, Orlando, FL (1990–1991)
Certification: Electronics Technician
- A seven-month course concentrating on electricity and electronics, communications systems, digital logic, microprocessor-based equipment, and radar.
- Training consisted of the study of how to interpret schematic diagrams and use appropriate test equipment as well as hands-on experience on how to isolate and correct faults in both military and civilian electronic equipment.

ELIZABETH A. MOLINA

5 Thornton Avenue ◆ Rockville Centre, New York 11570 ◆ (516) 573-6288
emolina@msn.com

PROFILE

Former educator with a record of fostering academic learning and enhancing students' critical thinking skills, *eager to return* to a **Social Studies Teacher** position. Utilize stimulating, artfully employed vocabulary to instruct students, and multisensory approach in presenting subject material. Versatile, solid experience with multiple intelligence school populations. Organized, accurate, and detail-oriented time-management skills. Partnered with community and business resources for the purpose of enhancing educational experience. Encourage strong inter-teacher cooperation and exchange of ideas. Maintain communication channels with parents.

*More recent credentials are
highlighted early in the resume*

CERTIFICATIONS

New York State Certificate of Qualification in Secondary Education Social Studies (7–12th), 2000
New York State Extension Certificate (5–6th), 2000
Red Cross First Aid Certification for Coaching / CPR for Coaching, 2000

*Older teaching experience
comes before current job
because
candi-
date
wants
to
return
to
teach-
ing*

PROFESSIONAL TEACHING EXPERIENCE

NORTH SHORE CENTRAL SCHOOL DISTRICT • Sea Cliff, NY   1990
Substitute Teacher / Social Studies, Grades Nine to Twelve • Assistant Varsity Track Coach
• Devised and implemented well-received lesson plans in Social Studies.
• Taught document-based questions.
• Established learning environments that met the intellectual, social, and creative needs of all students.
• Encouraged an atmosphere of active student participation.
• Provided tutoring services for students needing extra help.
• Related to a wide range of students/administration crossing cultural lines.

OYSTER BAY–EAST NORWICH SCHOOL DISTRICT • Oyster Bay, NY   1989
Substitute Teacher / Social Studies, High School • Assistant Football Coach
• Created and implemented innovative teaching methodologies, strategies, and instructional techniques.
• Formulated well-received lesson plans from the Civil War to World War II utilizing New York State Curriculum.
• Selected textbooks, videos, and research materials.
• Developed cooperative learning activities; evaluated unit exams.
• Provided tutoring for students needing extra help.
• Attended various faculty meetings and subject team meetings.

Submitted by Donna Farrise

ELIZABETH A. MOLINA
- Page Two -

MANHASSET SCHOOL DISTRICT • Centereach, NY   **1979 to 1980**
Substitute Teacher / Social Studies, High School • Assistant Spring Track Coach / Head Winter Track Coach
- Formulated unit plans and taught Social Studies and Government classes.
- Encouraged a learning atmosphere of active student participation.
- Challenged students to develop their own solutions to political problems.
- Provided group instruction and designed tests to evaluate student performance.
- Utilized group dynamics in assessing students.
- Supervised hall duties, study halls, and cafeteria duties.
- Attended multidisciplinary and faculty meetings, and parent-teacher conferences.

Legal career is downplayed **PROFESSIONAL EXPERIENCE**

O'HALLERAN, FRENCH, & WINTERS • Holtsville, NY   **6/90 to Present**
Associate Attorney • 8/93 to Present
Independently arbitrate, negotiate, and litigate all aspects of criminal, civil, family, negligence, and contractual cases. Areas of concentration include, but are not limited to: preparing all papers necessary for litigation, settlement, and processing of appeals.
- Perform client interviews; research information; draft affidavits, briefs, contracts, memoranda of law, and effect pleadings.
- Conduct discoveries, plan case strategies, and try jury trials to verdict.
- Analyze law sources; i.e., statutes, recorded judicial decisions, legal articles, treaties, constitutions, and legal codes.
- Supervise paralegal and legal secretarial staff.

Legal Assistant • 6/90 to 8/93

LICENSES

New York State Bar Association

MEMBERSHIPS / ASSOCIATIONS

American Bar Association
Suffolk Bar Association
New York State Bar Association
Association of Trial Lawyers of America (ATLA)

EDUCATION

New York University, New York, NY
Juris Doctor, 1993

St. John's University, Jamaica, NY
Bachelor of Arts in Liberal Arts, 1990

Andrea Charania

acharania@yahoo.com

3673 Bert Hill • Howell, Michigan 48844 • 810.229.6811

Professional Profile paints a perfect picture of who she is and what she is qualified for

PROFESSIONAL PROFILE

Well-qualified professional with advanced credentials and skilled at teaching, training, presenting, and advocating learning initiatives. Proven results in productivity/performance improvement initiatives. Proactive member of district, county, and state committees and programs. Quick learner in both independent and team-driven environments; disciplined work ethic. Competencies include

- Strategic Planning & Leadership
- Project/Program Development & Management
- Training Trainers
- Public Speaking

- Public and Community Relations
- Library Science
- Reading & Learning Initiatives
- Educational Programming

Equally strong qualifications in general management, organizational development, research, and human resource affairs. Extensive hands-on expertise with success at identifying and resolving issues.

Recognized by peers and recipient of "Teacher of the Year" in the district, 2001.

EDUCATION & TRAINING

Training is included in the education section, which illustrates her strong educational background

M.Ed. • 1993—Wayne State University
B.S. degree • 1980—Michigan State University

Certified Reading Specialist
Certified Auditory Verbal Therapist
Junior Class Learning of New Zealand
Trainer of Trainers
Developmental Examiner—Gesell Institute
Reading Recovery Training
Maintain certification through continuous education courses/programs

EXPERIENCE

BRIGHTON SCHOOL DISTRICT; Brighton, Michigan
Teacher • 1987–94, 1996–present
Instructor for all subjects (general elementary education) in the first through fifth grades; coach special education (hearing-impaired) students.
Trainer/Presenter • 1997–99
Led programs to train others in diverse learning strategies. Presented *Dimensions of Learning* program to professional teachers.
Teacher • 1980–82

LIVINGSTON COUNTY (MICHIGAN)
Advocate • 2000–01
Member of planning committee developing statewide initiatives for Michigan Literacy Program. Responsible for identifying and supporting favorable actions. Trained trainers in the program.
Project Leader • 2000
Headed countywide summer reading program.

Other Experience

"Other Experience" is highlighted to stand alone to showcase the importance of the position

WAYNE COUNTY (MICHIGAN)
Supervisor • 1994–96
Led Hearing Impaired Program; consulted on innovative reading initiatives.

Appointed to *STATE OF MICHIGAN GRANT COMMITTEE*; provided writing, reading, and rating for various grant proposals.

— *Excellent references available* —

Submitted by Lorie Lebert

Anna Maria Gomez

414 Acorn Court, Lawrenceville, NJ 08648
(609) 771-5555 ▪ marlem@earthlink.net

Spanish Teacher at the Middle or High School Level

Resume leads off with her Education and Certification, most relevant to the new career she is pursuing

EDUCATION & CERTIFICATION

New Jersey Teacher's Certification, Spanish K–12

BA, Spanish Language & Civilization / Teaching (cum laude), Rutgers University, New Brunswick, NJ
    ✓ Two semesters at University of Valencia, Spain. Summer study at University of Madrid.
MBA, International Business / Marketing, Columbia University, New York, NY

PROFILE *Profile showcases some of her unique qualifications and strengths*

☑ Fluent Spanish. Basic conversational Portuguese and good reading ability. Familiar with French.
☑ Experienced Spanish teacher with demonstrated track record of obtaining outstanding results, utilizing highly effective interpersonal and communications skills.
☑ Detail-oriented, analytical professional with proven organizational and problem solving abilities.
☑ Computer literate: Windows 2003, MS Word, Excel, Outlook, Print Shop, and Internet Explorer.

PROFESSIONAL EXPERIENCE *Transferable skills most relevant to teaching are highlighted under Professional Experience*

TEACHING / COMMUNICATIONS

▪ Designed Spanish-language curriculum and taught one 2½-hour class weekly for The Princeton Community School. Used text, multimedia, and visual aids to make classroom learning relevant to adults. Resulted in high re-registration rate for following semesters.

▪ Trained small groups of end users on computerized banking services for Mercantile Banking and Trust Company. Conducted product presentations and consultative interviews with clients and prospects. Created and implemented marketing plans for corporate clients in Latin America.

▪ Consulted with clients of International Research Corporation to determine specifications for customized market / opinion research projects. Wrote proposals and translated textbook chapters and questionnaires from Spanish to English. Developed marketing collaterals and account relationship management techniques to ensure top-notch company image and service.

ORGANIZATION / PROJECT MANAGEMENT

▪ Coordinated complex, multinational research projects for Research Analysis and International Research Corporation. Led and trained project teams and ensured timely completion of projects within budget.

▪ Coordinated translations from Spanish to English for scholarly magazine, obtaining and evaluating board member input on editorial content, all while meeting strict publication deadlines. Streamlined procedures for foreign-language advertisement and order fulfillment (Medical Learning Systems).

EMPLOYMENT HISTORY

Director of International Marketing	International Research Corp., Somerset, NJ	2000–2006
Spanish I Teacher	Princeton Community School, Princeton, NJ	1999–2004
Field Administrator	Research Analysis Corp., Skillman, NJ	1998–1999
Coordinator—Latin American Services	Medical Learning Systems, Skillman, NJ	1997–1998
Senior Marketing & Sales Rep.	Mercantile Banking and Trust Co., New York	previously

Submitted by Susan Guarneri

Paula Redford

1112 W. 73rd St., New York, NY 10023
212-555-5555
predford@xyz.com

SUMMARY

ESL/TOEFL Instructor with proven ability to teach adults of all levels of proficiency with varied educational and business backgrounds. Experience includes teaching conversational and written English. Knowledge of multiple cultures through travel and continuing contacts with people throughout Europe, Asia, South America, and Africa.

EXPERIENCE

Only the most recent and relevant jobs are included

ESL Instructor—New York Language Institute, New York, NY   1992–Present

- Teach ESL to private students and business executives; customize lessons according to occupation and level of English proficiency.
- Prepare students for the TOEFL exam.

ESL Instructor—Rutgers University   1992
Language Institute for English (L.I.F.E.) summer program at
The Juilliard School at Lincoln Center, New York, NY

- Taught specialized program for international musicians to improve English proficiency.

ESL and TOEFL Instructor—Pace University, New York, NY   1989–1991

- Taught ESL classes, from beginner to advanced levels, to American immigrants.

Previous experience includes positions as medical administrator at hospitals and for research programs, also tour guide and museum docent.

EDUCATION

B.A., *magna cum laude,* Columbia University, New York, NY   *Graduation date is omitted*

Graduate Studies:
New York University, teaching methodology and applied linguistics
New School for Social Research, language learning and teaching

License:
New York State Teacher's License #1234

Would you guess that this candidate is 81 years old? The word "retirement" is not in her vocabulary!

Submitted by Wendy Gelberg

John Belmont

978.555.8113

E-mail: jbelmont@aol.com

177 Washington Avenue • Boston, MA 95818

Sales Management

Heading doubles as an adjective

Delivering consistent and sustainable revenue gains, profit growth, and market-share increases through strategic sales leadership of multi-site branch locations. Valued offered:

✓ Driver of innovative programs that provide a competitive edge and establish company as a full-service market leader.
✓ Proactive, creative problem solver who develops solutions that save time, cut costs, and ensure consistent product quality.
✓ Empowering leader who recruits, develops, coaches, motivates, and inspires sales teams to top performance.
✓ Innovative in developing and implementing win-win solutions to maximize account expansion, retention, and satisfaction.

Selected Career Achievements

RANFORD COMPANY • Boston, MA   1990 to 2006

As Branch Manager, reinvigorated the sales organization, growing company revenues from $9MM to $45MM, expanding account base from 450 to 680, and increasing market share 15%. Established new performance benchmark and trained sales team on implementing sales-building customer inventory rationalization programs.

- **Revitalized and restored profitability of 2 underperforming territories** by coaching and developing territory reps.

- **Penetrated 2 new markets** and secured a lucrative market niche in abrasive products. Staffed, opened, and managed the 2 branch locations with 22 employees in New Jersey—both sites produced $19.5 MM+ over 3 years.

- **Initiated and advanced the skills of the sales force to effectively promote and sell increasingly technical product lines** in response to changing market demands.

Increased profit margins and dollar volume through product mix diversification and expansion. Created product catalogs and marketing literature.

- **Ensured that the company maintained its competitive edge in the marketplace** by adding several cross-functional product lines.

- **Led highly profitable new product introduction with a 40% profit margin** that produced $100K annually in new business.

Industry is not mentioned so that the candidate can apply to jobs in different industries

BERLIN COMPANY • Worcester, MA   1985 to 1990

As Account Executive, rejuvenated sales performance of a stagnant territory. Turned around customer perception by cultivating exceptional relationships through solutions-based selling and delivering value-added service. Recognized as a peak performer company-wide who consistently ranked #1 in sales and #1 in profits.

- **Positioned and established company as a full-service supplier** to drive sales revenues by translating customer needs to product solutions.

- **More than doubled territory sales from $700K to $1.6MM** during tenure and grew account base from 80 to 125 through new market penetration. **Landed and managed 3 of company's 6 largest accounts** and grew remaining 3.

- **Captured a lucrative account and drove annual sales from $100K in the first year to $400K in 3 years**—outperforming the competition without any price-cutting.

- **Mentored new and existing territory reps** on customer relationship management, solutions-selling strategies, advanced product knowledge, and customer programs.

Education

B.S. in Business Management—Rhode Island University, Providence, RI

Focus is on results rather than responsibilities

Submitted by Louise Garver

SHONYELL JOHNSON

123 Palm Street   St. Petersburg, Florida 33710   (727) 555-1212   E-mail: creativeone@knology.net

CAREER PROFILE

RESULTS-ORIENTED BUSINESS MANAGEMENT PROFESSIONAL with 10+ years of solid experience with small business ownership, education, and human services. Polished professional with a proven track record of success in strategic business planning, operations, relationship-partnering, sales, and vendor and community relations. Expertise in event planning, leadership development, mentoring, and case management. Former honors student who worked full-time while attending college full-time and maintaining volunteer activities in the community. Consistently exceed expectations on all job performance evaluations.

PROFESSIONAL OBJECTIVE

Seeking to contribute to a company's growth and profitability as a Business Development Specialist.

COMPUTER SKILLS

Windows 98, NT, Me & XP   Microsoft Office 2000 (Access, Excel, PowerPoint, & Word)
Microsoft Outlook   Microsoft Outlook Express   Internet Research
Proprietary Educational and Human Services Software

Recently earned business degree is featured close to the top, even though she has more than 10 years of work experience

EDUCATION

B.S., BUSINESS MANAGEMENT, ECKERD COLLEGE PROGRAM FOR EXPERIENCED LEARNERS, ST. PETERSBURG, FLORIDA (2006)
❖ **G.P.A.: 3.6 / 4.0**
❖ Worked full-time while attending college full-time.

COURSE HIGHLIGHTS

Accounting   Business Finance   Ethics in Management   Investment Finance
Management Leadership   Marketing   Microeconomics

A.A., ST. PETERSBURG COLLEGE, ST. PETERSBURG, FLORIDA
❖ Worked full-time while attending college full-time.

PROFESSIONAL EXPERIENCE

CO-OWNER, EBONY GUESS, ST. PETERSBURG, FLORIDA & ATLANTA, GEORGIA
❖ Full profit & loss responsibility for a successful music sales business with revenue topping **$300,000** annually.
❖ As co-owner, started the business from its inception and successfully grew it into a profitable venture in under one year.
❖ Handle all strategic planning, marketing, financial, and accounting duties associated with the business.
❖ Maintain extensive records of all business transactions and plan for conservative future growth.
❖ Thoroughly learned all policies, procedures, licensing, permit, small business regulations, requirements, and standards for opening a business.
❖ Joined the Chamber of Commerce and the Midtown Economic Development Council.

Submitted by Sharon McCormick

**STATE OF FLORIDA, DEPARTMENT OF HEATLH, HEALTHY FAMILIES PINELLAS / YWCA
ST. PETERSBURG, FLORIDA**
Family Support Worker (2001 to Present)
- ❖ Work as part of a nationwide organization with **400+** offices across the country for a program considered to be the most successful child-abuse-prevention outfit in the United States.
- ❖ Work with several highly respected agencies including the *YWCA, Healthy Families Pinellas, the Department of Health,* and the *State of Florida.*
- ❖ Establish a trusting relationship with the parents of children considered at-risk for abuse and neglect to help them create healthier family environments.
- ❖ Create a *"Family Support Plan"* with specific goals, objectives, and activities in conjunction with the Program Supervisor.
- ❖ Assist in strengthening the parent/child relationship through improving parenting skills and meeting the basic needs of the family with the goal of community resource integration and self-sufficiency.
- ❖ Provide in-home visits with prenatal and postnatal parents every week and follow up with the family for up to five years.
- ❖ Enthusiastically teach parenting education to culturally diverse families with cutting-edge materials created by the national organization.
- ❖ Complete precise documentation per the program's requirements and utilize the computer for case planning.
- ❖ Thoroughly learned extensive community resource information and make referrals as needed.
- ❖ Consistently *"Exceed Expectations"* on annual job performance evaluations.

PARENTS FOR CHILDREN PRESCHOOL, ST. PETERSBURG, FLORIDA
Assistant Director (1998 to 2001)
- ❖ Performed human resources functions, including recruiting, hiring, coaching, supervising, disciplining, and terminating staff.
- ❖ Handled administrative office responsibilities for the preschool.
- ❖ Provided direct service to the children in classroom settings.
- ❖ Acted as a liaison for the children with professionals in the community as needed.
- ❖ Praised by parents for excellence in educational instruction with their children.
- ❖ Accepted more challenging position with the State of Florida.

GREAT BEGINNINGS PRE-SCHOOL, ST. PETERSBURG, FLORIDA
Teacher (1993 to 1996)
- ❖ Promoted a positive classroom setting for children by utilizing education and play activities.
- ❖ Prepared comprehensive lesson plans targeted toward different learning styles.
- ❖ Provided guidance, direction, understanding, and comfort to the children as needed.
- ❖ Accepted more responsible position at the Parents for Children Preschool.

VOLUNTEER EXPERIENCE

BROOKWOOD YOUNG WOMEN'S RESIDENCE, ST. PETERSBURG, FLORIDA
Volunteer (2005 to 2006)
- ❖ Acted as a *Mentor* to up **50** troubled teenagers for a local young women's residential facility.
- ❖ Assisted with character-building and leadership-development activities for the teenagers.
- ❖ Praised by top management for communication and interpersonal skills with the residents.

LAKEWOOD HIGH SCHOOL, ST. PETERSBURG, FLORIDA
Volunteer (2004 to 2005)
- ❖ Acted as a *Mentor* to teenagers at a local high school with **1,000+** students.

REFERENCES AVAILABLE UPON REQUEST

Sam R. Wilson

3720 Broadview Terrace
Cedarville, OH 45314

s6496889@yahoo.com

(937) 641-0018 (Home)
(937) 649-6889 (Cell)

SALES & MANAGEMENT

Food Industry

Focus statement quickly summarizes the candidate's experience and tells how a company can benefit from hiring him

FOCUS

Management professional with a distinguished 16-year career that will benefit gross margin improvement, comparable store sales, teamwork productivity, and effective merchandising.

SALES & MANAGING EXPERIENCE

Operations Manager — *Pete's Meat Market*, Cedarville, OH   10/2005–03/2006

- Directed training, merchandising, and department sets.
- Category management of the entire market prior to opening.
- Directly responsible for $290K in sales the first 2 months of business.
- Weekly sales increases the first 10 weeks of 2006.
- Established and cultivated positive vendor relations.

Store Manager — *Stop 'n' Go Market*, Cedarville, OH   1999–2005

- Increased wine sales 150% from 2000–2005.
- Increased net profits by 3% per annum beginning in 2001.
- Sales growth of 15% from 2002–2005.

Store Director — *Jerry's Food Markets*, Cedarville, OH   1998–1999

- Reduced backroom inventory $100K in first quarter of 1998.
- Consistently exceeded company sales and gross profit objectives.
- Effectively supervised 8 department managers and over 100 employees.
- Reduced labor costs from 8.1% to 6.1% to add to bottom-line profits.

Job titles are easy to read due to use of boldfacing, indents, and white space

Meat Department Manager—*Jerry's Food Markets*, Cedarville, OH   1990–1997

- Exceeded gross profit and labor objectives consistently.
- Highest-volume meat department with 10% sales increases annually.
- Acted as interim store manager in absence of market directors.

EDUCATION

- **Spartan Foods Training Courses 1991–1999:** "Wings of the Future," "Sanitation," "Positive Discipline," "Effective Time Management," "Leadership," "Department Sales Growth," and "Merchandising"

- **Zig Zigler "See You At the Top" Motivational Seminar,** 1997 — graduated first in class

Submitted by Terry Ferrara

This senior executive needed **JOHN J. MONLEY**
a resume quickly to give   236 Kings Hwy. • Darien, CT 06820
                               203.655.2444 Res • 203.355.4323 Cell • jmonley@gmail.com
*to a recruiter who called unexpectedly, so the writer focused on key highlights and kept
the resume to one page* **FINANCIAL SERVICES EXECUTIVE**

Senior Managing Director with more than 30 years of consistent success in the highly volatile fixed income markets. Excel in developing strategies and techniques to manage interest rate risk.

Recognized as Top 3 in production nationwide every year for 26 years.

Earned 100% client retention rate over 26 years by providing savvy guidance and market expertise.

Effective Strategist who blends technical acumen and market insight to develop effective hedging and investing strategies.

Honest, ethical leader with the highest level of integrity. Recognized for expert knowledge of regulatory rules and procedures.

PROFESSIONAL EXPERIENCE

MERRILL LYNCH ✧ NEW YORK, NY   **1979–PRESENT**

SENIOR MANAGING DIRECTOR, FIXED INCOME AND MUNICIPALS ✧ 1985–PRESENT

Successively promoted to positions of increased responsibility based on consistently exceeding goals and expectations.

➢ *Started institutional practice* targeting middle market financial services firms. Assisted in developing client base through effective financial/portfolio analysis, tax swapping, trading, and investment strategies.

➢ Promoted to move to Chicago to run Institutional sales team. (1985–2004). *Increased Chicago sales revenue 100% for each of first 2 years.*

➢ *Top 3 in production every year for 26 years.*

➢ *Earned #1 rank for performance in 23 of 26 years.*

➢ Became co-national sales manager in 1995 to improve performance of national sales force of 20. *Restructured organization and dramatically improved efficiencies* and client communications for fixed-income accounts.

➢ Recognized for introducing techniques in structured products and hedging instruments to improve returns and management of risk.

LF ROTHCHILD ✧ NEW YORK, NY ✧ ASSOCIATE ✧ 1976–1979

EDUCATION

BS, Banking & Finance
Saint Johns University ✧ New York
Won numerous awards for Economics & Finance

Submitted by Don Goodman

This combination resume highlights functional skills and achievements on page 1

KATIE N. ANDERSON

1456 Apple Blossom Drive • Savannah, GA 31401
(912) 123-4567 • knanderson@abc.net

OPERATIONS EXECUTIVE

Highly motivated executive with more than 20 years of experience in contract administration, quality assurance, and new product development. Principal customer industries: procedure trays; boundary product; examination gloves; and federal, state, and local governments. Adept at analysis and business re-engineering, increasing bottom-line revenues and gross profits. Proven performer in recruitment and management encompassing personnel, contract negotiations, and customer relations. Areas of expertise include

➢ Operations & Materials Management	➢ Purchasing Operations
➢ Cost Controls & Reductions	➢ Sales & Marketing Management
➢ Market Share Strategies	➢ Vendor Management
➢ Major Client Management	➢ Organizational Development
➢ Competitive Maneuvering	➢ Staff Development

OPERATIONS MANAGEMENT ACHIEVEMENTS

➢ Directed streamlining of multiple production sites to ultimately reduce shipping costs and increase gross profit margins 45%.

➢ Recruited to "clean house" and begin again. Re-engineered production planning, procurement, quality assurance, distribution, and sales administration departments. Increased overall productivity by 20%.

➢ Created product management system, which accelerated pricing, contract negotiations, and distribution agreements; increased profits by 27% through cost reductions and control.

➢ Negotiated multibillion-dollar group contract, which had been suspended for three years. Developed pricing strategy and fee payment program that overshot the competing bid by 15%, yet maintaining 20% gross profit.

➢ Generated $25M multiyear savings and accelerated productivity growth through development of private-brand products.

Submitted by Tammy Chisholm

A brief summary of professional experience appears on page 2

Katie N. Anderson   Page 2 of 2

PROFESSIONAL EXPERIENCE

Xidus Medical, Inc.—Savannah, GA   1997–2005
Ranked among the top medical manufacturers, offers broad spectrum of boundary and custom procedure try products.
Vice President, Operations
Managed plant production and sales requirements while overseeing planning, scheduling, sales, quality control, and distribution. Direct 15 managers and 10 engineers with national P&L accountability.

Divad Custom Procedure Trays—Savannah, GA   1976–1997
$1B leading national custom procedure tray manufacturer and distributor.
Director, Sales Administration (1993–1997)
Oversaw sales representative alignments, corporate account fee calculation/ distribution, and product catalog. Developed cost reduction and gross profit acceleration system for slow-moving product, increasing sales 54%.

Manager, Marketing & Sales Services (1976–1993)
Directed 50 sales and customer service representatives. Managed and trained sales representatives in custom procedure tray contents and sterilization methods. Developed and implemented bid and analysis processes to maximize profit and revenue growth.

EDUCATION

Master of Business Administration
The Wharton School, University of Pennsylvania, Philadelphia, PA

Bachelor of Science in Business
Virginia Commonwealth University, Richmond, VA

ORGANIZATIONS

Executive Board, United Way
Vice Chairman, Savannah Habitat for Humanity Chapter
Board Member, Hanover County Red Cross and Zoning Commission

This resume emphasizes transferable skills because she is changing careers

Kendall Rose

811 66th Avenue North
Myrtle Beach, SC 29572

krose@yahoo.com

Home (555) 555-5555
Cell (555) 555-5555

FOCUS: PHARMACEUTICAL SALES

Medical professional with a full understanding of the complexities of the healthcare field and insight into medical decision-making

Professional Profile

- Able to establish productive relationships and foster credibility with a variety of healthcare professionals

- Skilled at documenting and communicating complex technical information in a nontechnical manner

- Accustomed to a high-pressure work environment that demands careful and meticulous attention to detail

"People skills" are important for a pharmaceutical sales rep, so they are featured up front

Medical Knowledge / Qualifications

- Offering first-hand knowledge of clinical applications and a strong background in treatment-related medical services *Medical knowledge is also important*

- Well-versed in treatment planning & medical terminology and exposed to a variety of medications and conditions *in this profession*

- Demonstrated ability to quickly grasp scientific information and rapidly master new skills

HIGHLIGHTS OF QUALIFICATIONS

→ High-performance individual with a self-motivated working style and strong critical-thinking skills. Able to work independently and function effectively with multidisciplinary teams from all areas of an organization.

→ Experience reflects a consistent record of success for anticipating problems and finding creative solutions while exhibiting superior judgment *and* a balanced, realistic understanding of issues.

→ Competent and well-spoken with a confident professional presence, engaging interpersonal skills, and a proven ability to communicate effectively and persuasively with diverse personalities in various situations.

→ Prepared to meet the expectations of the most demanding physicians through a highly accessible service orientation and rigorous followup. Capable of educating healthcare professionals about the efficacy and safety of medical products.

PROFESSIONAL EXPERIENCE

Grand Strand Hospital, *Myrtle Beach, SC*   **1991 to Present**
Medical Radiation Dosimetrist (1995 to Present)
Prepare and administer radiation treatment plans, which requires the performance of simulations, dose calculations, and tolerance-limit determinations. Perform specific measurements and provide data for treatment plans, adhering to a quality-assurance program. Assist radiation oncologists during simulations to ensure appropriate treatment plans and calculate distribution of doses for radiation therapy treatments. Follow the most current protocol and utilize a treatment planning system. Review patient charts and inspect treatment records to ensure accuracy. Provide guidance and direction to treatment therapists.

Chief Therapist (1991 to 1995)
Supervised technical staff, patient treatment, patient simulation, simulation scheduling, and quality assurance. Accountable for dosimetry coverage, custom blocking, film approval, staffing, machine coverage, and payroll. Developed and documented new QA procedures and maintained services in accordance with hospital, state, local, and federal standards. Implemented other routine QA activities in the calibration of linear accelerators and dosimetry equipment.

Submitted by Kristin Coleman

Kendall Rose   **Page Two**

PROFESSIONAL EXPERIENCE continued...

Mohawk Valley Community Hospital, *Utica, NY*   **1988 to 1991**
Chief Therapist / Department Supervisor
Responsible for the daily operation of the Radiation Oncology area, which included the overall supervision of clerical and technological staff. Maintained departmental policies and procedures, objectives, safety, environmental, and infection-control standards. Established and maintained the quality-assurance program. Served on the Radiation Safety committee and as coordinator of oncology nursing programs and continuing-education programs.

St. Agnes Hospital, *White Plains, NY*   **1982 to 1984**
Staff Radiation Therapist
Delivered prescribed and planned course of radiation therapy to patients, obtained patient history, answered questions, and explained procedure. Interfaced extensively with physician and radiation oncologist. Reinforced recommendations given to patient by the physicians regarding reaction to treatment, care of the radiated area, and local side effects.

Westchester Medical Center, *Valhalla, NY*   **1981 to 1982**
Staff Radiation Therapist
Provided skilled technical performance for delivery of radiotherapeutic treatments, as prescribed by the radiation oncologist. Accountable for patient treatments, simulation, filming, and student orientation/supervision. Acquired dosimetry experience.

EDUCATION / CREDENTIALS

University of South Carolina, *Columbia, SC*   **Certification**
Associate Degree in Radiologic Technology   AIDS

Licensures
Registered Radiation Therapist, American Registry of Radiologic Technologists
Certified Radiologic Technologist—Radiotherapy

PROFESSIONAL DEVELOPMENT

Clinical Equipment   **Clinical Treatment Planning Systmes**
➤ Various Simulators   ➤ Eclipse
➤ Varian Treatment Machines   ➤ Theraplan
➤ Siemens Treatment Machines   ➤ Render Plan

Professional Affiliation
➤ American Society of Radiologic Technologists (ASRT)

149

Mariah Masterson

9 Prospect Drive, Portland, ME 01069
mariahmast@yahoo.com / (417) 834-1429 (c) ● (417) 665-4345 (h)

CAREER PROFILE:

Text is indented so that headings stand out to the reader

Highly motivated media sales professional seeking a challenging position where my skills and abilities will have maximum impact. Qualifications include

- Dedicated to superior customer service
- Proven track record of new business development
- High sales producer who consistently exceeds goals
- Resourceful problem solver with excellent organizational ability
- Outstanding communication, interpersonal, and self-management skills
- Strong team leader able to set high standards and motivate others to excel

EXPERIENCE:

Account Executive, Time Warner Cable, Portland, ME (2002–present)
Responsible for customizing campaigns for clients, selling airtime on 31 insertable cable networks, script writing, trafficking commercials as ordered, and keeping all billing at NET 30. Maintain and upsell current client base and manage aggressive new business development.
Accomplishments:

Bullets are used sparingly to keep from diminishing their impact

- Named to "The President's Club" for outstanding sales for first year with the company.
- Generated a 65% increase of new business on client list over the past three years.
- Met and exceeded monthly and annual sales goals: Exceeded first annual budget by 24%.

Account Executive, New World Media, *The Daily Planet,* Portland, ME (1999–2002)
Responsible for selling advertising space in four regional alternative newsweeklies. Daily tasks included face-to-face client presentations, booking space and designing ads, gathering info from clients to meet space deadlines while maintaining the best collections in the office. Worked within clients' budgets to execute campaigns based on their needs cycle and balanced that with the policies of the company. Represented *The Daily Planet* at various business and social functions.
Accomplishments: *"Accomplishments" subheadings allow the candidate to*

- Managed a large client base and brought 55% new business to the paper. *showcase special*
- Exceeded sales goals by average of 21% during tenure. *contributions*

Account Executive, WHCN, Madison, WI (1996–1999)
Responsible for bringing in new business as well as servicing and growing existing account base. Wrote commercial copy and produced spots; coordinated talent, effects, and input from clients. Kept collections current, routed traffic, and designed individual promotions and campaigns based on clients' needs and market research.
Accomplishment:

- Increased new business by 60% during tenure with the station.

EDUCATION:

University of Wisconsin, Madison, WI (1993)
Bachelor of Arts: Business Management

REFERENCES: Available upon request

Submitted by Mary Hayward

Al Marchano
entry-level commercial
real estate professional

25 Crane Road
Center, Alabama 36000
334.555.5555 (home) – 334.555.6666 (cell)
almarch1111@hotmail.com

WHAT I CAN OFFER ACME PROPERTIES

❑ The drive and skill to build and **maintain a "pipeline" of potential deals.**

❑ The **personal contacts** among **key decision makers statewide,** including bankers, mayors, city council members, and elected officials.

❑ The **vision to see** and **close deals** others have **overlooked.**

RECENT AND RELEVANT WORK HISTORY WITH EXAMPLES OF PROBLEMS SOLVED

❑ **Majority Owner,** Standard Builders, LLC, Centerville, Alabama   Jul 04–Present
H&E serves the tri-county area building spec homes 1,800ft² and larger.

The results of each story are placed first

BUILDING RELATIONSHIPS WITH KEY PLAYERS IN COMMERCIAL REAL ESTATE

Used my personal contact to persuade a banker to extend a major capital venture loan. Overcame a lack of a professional track record in building and partner's limited credit scores to prove we were a good financial risk. *Payoffs:* Loan **approved** in just two months.

❑ Major, Alabama Army National Guard, serving in a variety of assignments with increasing responsibility in Alabama and Saudi Arabia   Mar 89–Present

FINDING AND SERVING CUSTOMERS OTHERS HAVE OVERLOOKED

Turned around a product that customers didn't like—even though they were a "captive" market: a corporate newspaper. Recruited the right people to help me. Then went to where our readers lived to see what they wanted. Finally, overcame management's resistance to change to roll out an entirely new product. *Payoffs:* **Increased** circulation **by 100 percent.** We were pressed to keep up with customer demand—the strongest it had been in years.

Bold print guides the reader's eyes to payoffs they can use

TURNING DIVERSE GROUPS INTO SOLID SUPPORTERS

Went beyond changing the group I was asked to lead from dissatisfied strangers into a smoothly running team. Listened carefully, and then built their trust through demonstrated fairness every day. *Payoffs:* **Retention grew 15 percentage points. Met** my **goals** in this area for **30 consecutive months**—a rare feat.

❑ **District Director** *and* **Campaign Manager,** Office of Congressman Conrad Morton, Montgomery, Alabama   Mar 96–Dec 96 and Dec 01–Jan 02

BUILDING COALITIONS AMONG PEOPLE WHO DRIVE COMMERCIAL REAL ESTATE

Helped our candidate dominate the field by reaching out—personally—to mayors, city council members, and business leaders. Gave them clear and compelling proof

*More indicators of performance **Acme Properties** can use …*

(continued)

Submitted by Don Orlando

(continued)

Al Marchano **Entry-Level Commercial Real Estate Professional** 334.555.5555

that we were ready and able to meet their needs. ***Payoffs:*** Not only did we build solid support, we came across so powerfully that **not one competitor** from our party **entered the race.**

❑ **Executive Director**, Alabama Republican Party, Foley, Alabama   Aug 97–Dec 98

Subheadings let readers jump to the stories most relevant to their needs

PERSUADING BUSINESS LEADERS TO INVEST IN THEIR FUTURE

Found a better way to raise money that aligned our requirements with the business community's needs. Called on committees (you would call them sales forces) in every one of Alabama's 67 counties. Motivated each one to ask businesses to donate goods and services in a fund-raising auction. Drove nearly 4,000 miles in just nine days to make these "warm calls." ***Payoffs:*** **From plan to results—from $100K in the red to $110K in the black—in just five months.**

EDUCATION AND PROFESSIONAL DEVELOPMENT

❑ BS, **Business Administration,** Troy University at Montgomery   91
Granted two leadership scholarships under a competitive program that recognized top performers. Earned this degree while working up to 20 hours a week and carrying a full academic load at night.

❑ AS, **Business Administration,** Alexander City Junior College, Alexander City, Alabama   86
Granted a one-year scholarship. Held down a 20-hour-a-week job. Served as both Student Government Association Treasurer and Class President.

❑ **"How to Generate Leads, Make Cold Calls, and Close Sales,"** Thomas Nelson, one week   04

COMPUTER SKILLS

❑ An expert in Word and Adobe Photoshop; comfortable with advanced Internet search protocols; working knowledge of Excel

LICENSES

❑ Alabama Real Estate License   Granted October 04

COMMUNITY AFFILIATIONS

❑ Member and Treasurer, Sigma Chi, Montgomery Chapter   86–Present
❑ Former member of the Centerville Rotary Club   01
❑ Former member of Centerville Kiwanis   95

Page 2

ALLAN WILDER

212-476-0090 allanwilderpro@comcast.net

22 Rood Street
Bronxville, NY 11100

Target job title is used as a heading for the profile section

MARKET RESEARCH ANALYST

Fast-track professional with more than six years of experience in conducting market research and analysis on electronic products in international markets. Key strengths lie in brand labeling, strategic sales planning, and client relationship management. Technically proficient with Microsoft Office and DTP software. Fluent in Japanese and conversant in German.

Representative Achievements:

Representative achievements immediately show that this young

✓ Recognized by Japan's leading economic magazine, *Outstanding Business Practices,* by winning the 2001 New Business Plan Award for pioneering new-market penetration matrix.

✓ First and youngest-ever company representative to earn coveted MVP award for playing pivotal role in launch of a new hand-held data set that outperformed sales forecasts by 25%.

✓ Acted as liaison between Japanese headquarters and newly formed U.S. branch that enabled North American markets to exceed benchmark goals.

candidate has already accomplished some impressive feats during his short career

PROFESSIONAL EXPERIENCE

PROFILES PLUS, New York, NY

2000 to Present

Marketing Representative and Coordinator, North America (2003 to Present)

Conduct market research and analysis, including brand recognition and technology trends; determine marketing strategy for North American sector. Develop new sales channels in United States; establish pricing, planning, and sales promotion tools. Design advertisements and exhibitions with media agency publishers. Analyze market needs; serve as a liaison to Japanese headquarters.

Introductory phrases of each achievement are boldfaced to emphasize the impact and scope of what he has achieved

- **Fast tracked to position as the most junior person in the company's history** to land promotion prior to completing five-year track at the assistant level.

- **Researched and uncovered new market segments that helped the company capture the #2 position** in the industry within only six months. Forged strong relations with new business partners that minimized competitive threat.

- **Created a branding strategy that enabled the sales force to tap into new marketplaces** and effectively positioned the subsidiary for triple-digit growth over a five-year period.

Sales & Promotion Marketing Assistant, International Division (2000–2003)

Created a unified user database for the overseas market and introduced a product modification plan that transformed hard-copy manuals into online references. Prepared presentation materials; organized Asian distributor meetings. Maintained meeting notes and agendas for distribution company-wide. Helped to analyze market trends and research new opportunities. Assisted with new product sales collateral.

- **Asked by senior management team to participate in a presentation on innovative marketing strategies** for post-Y2K in the electronics markets internationally.

- **Oriented and trained new marketing interns,** which resulted in the placement of four new professionals globally within eight months.

EDUCATION

INTERNATIONAL UNIVERSITY, Osaka, Japan—**Bachelor of Arts in Marketing,** 1999

Submitted by Jill Grindle

A two-column format allows for easy review of his qualifications

The profile positions him for the director level in terms of management, leadership, and administration

PETER BARISHNOVIC

678 MOUNTAIN VIEW ROAD
SEATTLE, WASHINGTON 98101
206.555.5877
PETERB@PROTYPELTD.COM

EXPERTISE

Demonstrated proficiency in the development of unique circus-arts techniques as well as educational program design, development, and management.

TECHNICAL SKILLS

International circus arts performer adept in
juggling,
balancing,
hat manipulation,
acrobatics,
aerial acrobatics,
trapeze,
wire walking,
teeterboard,
rolling globe,
unicycle,
clowning, and
magic.

EDUCATION

School for Ballet and Circus Arts, Volgograd, Russia

Completed degree program in Classical Ballet, specializing in Acrobatic Skills

AFFILIATIONS

Actors' Guild of Variety Artists

DUAL CITIZENSHIP

United States
Russian

LANGUAGE FLUENCY

English
Russian
French
Spanish

INTERNATIONAL CIRCUS ARTS DIRECTOR

CREATOR, INSTRUCTOR, AND DIRECTOR OF CIRCUS-ARTS PROGRAMS IN EDUCATIONAL INSTITUTIONS AND CORPORATE ENVIRONMENTS WORLDWIDE.

➤ Innovator of teaching methodology to maximize students' potential, strengths, and self-confidence.

➤ Talented trainer and coach who has developed students of all ages.

➤ Award-winning member of the Volzisky Troupe performing worldwide with the Brothers Benson Circus.

➤ Invited as guest instructor and consultant at the renowned International Clown College to train future performers.

The Accomplishments section reinforces the depth of his competencies

ACCOMPLISHMENTS

• Initiated and expanded circus-arts education program at Washington University that doubled revenues in just 2 years.

• Designed workshops, trained staff, and coordinated circus-arts program for major corporations throughout the world.

• Instructed and developed numerous students who achieved success as celebrated performers in international circus programs.

• Created and performed peerless juggling acts, including "Unsupported Ladder" and Musical Drum Juggling, with internationally acclaimed Volzhskiy Troupe.

• Directed development of the successful Big Top circus program, an annual event for the past 15 years.

• Multiple award winner for "Best Performing Act" in the European World Circus Competition and Cirque Atarré.

PROFESSIONAL EXPERIENCE

WASHINGTON UNIVERSITY • Seattle, Washington • 1989 to present
Assistant Director of Circus-Arts Program

Design and implement circus-arts instructional programs at the university. Recruit, supervise, and train instructors, building department from a staff of 3 to 10. Plan and manage program's operating budget. Coordinate instruction schedule and related activities; maintain and purchase equipment. Initiated design and implementation of effective safety standards for program.

SCHOOL FOR BALLET AND CIRCUS ARTS • Volgograd, Russia • 1980 to 1989
Circus Instructor

Created and instructed circus-arts program for students ranging from 7 to 18 years old. Developed and advanced the careers of numerous students who subsequently performed internationally.

CONSULTING EXPERIENCE: As consultant, provide expertise in the design and presentation of circus-arts workshops. Develop in-house trainers in creating circus productions to develop individual skills and promote teamwork (1989 to present).

PRIOR PERFORMING EXPERIENCE: International circus arts performer with the Volzhskiy Troupe, specializing in unique acrobatic/juggling acts.

Submitted by Louise Garver

KAREN B. EVERSLEY

9145 Ellicott Court, Manassas, VA 20111
Residence: 703-487-8541 ◊ Cellular: 703-458-7478 ◊ E-mail: keversley@yahoo.com

SENIOR EDITOR / WRITER

QUALIFICATIONS PROFILE

☐ **Internal & External Communications:** Ten-plus years of experience creating compelling articles, marketing materials, promotional documents, and trade publications; recent experience in Web content / online editing.

☐ **Publications:** Prolific author with wide cross-section of articles and feature stories published in magazines, Web sites, and industry journals.

☐ **Web Portfolio:** Visually appealing, interactive presentation of written work, including cutting-edge stories, news features and special projects at *www.kareneversley.net.* ◄——*Draws attention to a Web portfolio the candidate created*

☐ **Team Player:** Adept at building effective working relationships with content programmers, photo editors, promotion managers, and publishing staff.

☐ **Technical Skills:** Mac, PC, Word, WordPerfect, QuarkXPress, Photoshop, Illustrator, Dreamweaver, Flash, Adobe Photoshop for Newspapers, and Avid Xpress Pro.

Education is listed early because she has a new Master's degree relevant to her job target

EDUCATION & CERTIFICATIONS

MA in Interactive Journalism—American University, Washington, DC (2006)
BA in Public Communication—State University of New York College at Buffalo, NY (1994)
Federal Communications Commission (FCC) License (1989)

Hands-on experience and academic training in

- Advanced Editing
- Marketing Materials
- Press Releases
- Layout & Design
- Headline Writing

- Article/Feature Writing
- Digital Storytelling
- Brochures
- Web Content Creation
- Online Editing

- Public Speaking
- Multimedia Reporting
- In-depth Journalism
- Proofreading
- Promotional Copy

- Print Media
- Newsletter Creation
- Web Studio
- Online Publications
- Newspapers/Magazines

PROFESSIONAL EXPERIENCE

Editor, America Online, Dulles, VA (2005 to present)

- Serve as copy editor for high-traffic interactive company Web site with approximately 20 million paid subscribers and hits from 35 million visitors daily.

- Revise and edit "raw" script content into concise, audience-appropriate copy for major topics and events, including health, entertainment, commerce, and movies.

- Attend production and bimonthly network meetings to discuss upcoming promotions and special events; contribute unique story ideas to boost Web site readership.

- Support production managers to ensure smooth transition in Web content display and monitor deadlines.

Editor, American Newspaper Association, Vienna, VA (2003 to 2005)

- Translated broad information from wide variety of sources, including field experts and phone/e-mail questionnaires into engaging feature articles for bimonthly trade publication, *Newspaper Marketing,* reaching 5,000+ readers.

- Compiled and reviewed submissions from freelancers, colleagues, and other contributors to create editorial calendar; facilitated blue line, page count, and final print production.

- Played key role in the upgrade and redesign of magazine from layout, color selections, and font size; worked closely with senior vice president and creative services department.

(continued)

Submitted by Abby Locke

(continued)

KAREN B. EVERSLEY   PAGE TWO

PROFESSIONAL EXPERIENCE, continued

Marketing Coordinator, A+ Marketing Solutions, Fairfax, VA (2001 to 2003)

- Authored profile stories, "how-to," and trend feature pieces for international industry publications, *les nouvelles, esthetiques,* and *DERMASCOPE.*
- Developed full range of marketing and publicity documents—media pitch letters, press releases, brochures, banners, and direct mail; wrote copy for special events.

Communications/Events Director, Harpers Golf & Country Club, Sterling, VA (1999 to 2001)

- Managed corporate communications for community of more than 1,500 residents and club members.
- Launched monthly newsletter, *The Harpers Horn,* and grew publication from 4-page pamphlet to large size, 24-page color publication; enhanced publication with graphics and encouraged advertisements from local businesses.
- Contributed and wrote main articles; edited entire publication and oversaw entire print production process.

Public Affairs Assistant, Northern Virginia Association of Realtors, Fairfax, VA (1997 to 1998)

- Researched current industry events and issues, conducted interviews, and wrote relevant articles for monthly trade publication, *Realtor Keys,* which served more than 13,000 regional Realtors.

Corporate Communications Assistant, Fannie Mae, Washington, DC (1994 to 1997)

Positions on page 2 outline only the writing parts of these jobs

AFFILIATIONS & MEMBERSHIPS

The Online News Association
American Writers Association

Additional portfolio of writing samples available upon request.

KAREN B. EVERSLEY

9145 Ellicott Court, Manassas, VA 20111
Residence: 703-487-8541 ◊ Cellular: 703-458-7478 ◊ E-mail: keversley@yahoo.com

—Resume Addendum—

ONLINE ARTICLES / PRINT PUBLICATIONS

The resume addendum serves as a central place for listing her writing accomplishments and helps to dispel any perception that she is an underexperienced editor

THE AMERICAN OBSERVER:

- House Bill, FBI Target Gang Violence
- Dentists Close Your Eyes
- Penny Pinching Turns Pastime

YOGA PARADISE:

- The Heavenly Stretch

NEWSPAPER MARKETING:

- Using Mobile Technology to Reach Young Readers, an International Perspective
- Are You Missing Out? The Rapidly Growing Hispanic Community
- Transformation of Advertising, Knowing and Understanding Your Competitor's Future
- Halt Declining Readership
- Audio and Video Streaming, Advanced Features Sure to Attract New Readers and Advertisers (cover story)

DERMASCOPE:

- Beat the Summer Slump
- Haircare 101

LES NOUVELLES ESTHETIQUES:

- A Little Advice, One Owner's Business Plan

CELEBRITY CUTS:

- Ellie.Ellie Salon, Star Treatment

M WOMAN:

- Wife Rights

THE NVAR UPDATE:

- Photo spread with captions
- How to Profit from International Real Estate (cover story)
- How to Become a Real Estate Mentor (sidebar)

Kristina R. Hill

1228 Cedar Ridge Avenue □ White Marsh, MD 21162
(301) 555-5019 – Home □ (240) 555-2735 – Cell □ krh@msn.com

Job Target
Value
Offered

Receptionist □ Customer Service □ Office Support

♦ *Personable and friendly; good conversationalist, with excellent face-to-face and telephone communication skills.*

♦ *Active listener who demonstrates an innate ability to ask the right questions at the right time.*

♦ *Task oriented with an ability to balance strong interpersonal skills with need for efficiency.*

♦ *Down-to-earth and practical; place high value on following procedures.*

Mentions her ability to learn computer applications on her own

♦ *Patient, persistent, and diplomatic while providing explanations.*

♦ *Extremely attentive to detail and producing high-quality work.*

♦ *Methodical about gathering information and data to present logical and systematic approaches to completing tasks.*

♦ *Artistic and creative; keen sense of style, balance, and use of color.*

♦ *Computer literate with self-taught skills in Windows XP, Internet, e-mail, basic word processing, and keyboarding.*

Employment
History

Explains the time she was out of the workforce to raise children

Gained cross-functional office and customer service experience through various short-term positions while raising family and maintaining household (mid- 1980s and 1990s.)

♦ *Supported business office operations for* **Rich Lighting.** *Managed incoming calls, assisted customers in selecting lighting fixtures, operated cash register, verified credit purchases, and tracked product inventory.*

♦ *Demonstrated and sold new and used cars for* **Bowman Chevrolet.** *Provided customers with information about vehicle features and benefits; completed extensive paperwork; set-up and maintained account filing system; prospected for new business by phone and mail solicitation.*

♦ *Took over store management for Hagerstown branch of* **Carpet Town,** *including opening and closing responsibilities; customer service and sales; securing customer financing and calculating interest rates; office filing; and scheduling of installation projects.*

♦ *Answered phones, set-up filing system, and helped organize office for a newly established restaurant/pub.*

♦ *Created and sold hand-drawn greeting cards. Designed and distributed monthly newsletter for Williamsport Amvets Post. Designed covers for high school graduation and baccalaureate pamphlets.*

Education

Graduate, **Wye Mills High School,** *Wye Mills, MD*

Vocational Studies, **Commercial Art,** *Career Studies Center, Wye Mills, MD*

Submitted by Norine Dagliano

Strong fonts and aggressive writing indicate the candidate's modern style and forward-thinking approach

JULI STOLSON

824 BALSAM DRIVE, APEX, AZ 85365
(623) 972-0786   JSTOL@AOL.COM   CELL: (623) 506-4679

PROFILE

States what she can do and who she can do it for

Available to handle internal human resource, accounting, and payroll duties for a small to mid-sized company. Analytical, outgoing, and organized employee who learns quickly, works well under pressure, and is attentive to detail.

Strong analytical and mathematical aptitude. Motto of "get it done, and get it done right," combined with high degree of accuracy and organizational talents. Outstanding communication skills used in answering questions/inquiries, doing research, and resolving issues. Demonstrate the spirit of helping others and "going the extra mile" when needed.

Excited by the challenge of learning new fields, procedures, and systems. Currently completing accounting degree.

Three-column format draws reader's eye to her many talents

Customer Service	General Accounting	Quality Assurance
Human Resources	Bookkeeping	Bank Reconciliations
Payroll Processing	Taxes	Financial Statements
New Hires	Invoice / Client Billing	General Ledger
Terminated Employees	Spreadsheets	Word Processing
Writing	Government Agencies	Project Management

PROFESSIONAL EXPERIENCE

SENIOR PAYROLL SPECIALIST
ADP CHECK PROCESSING
PHOENIX, AZ   (2002–PRESENT)

Process client payrolls and resolve issues for this leading national provider of payroll, human resource, and benefits outsourcing solutions for small to medium-sized businesses. Manage more than 250 clients processing weekly, bi-weekly, semi-monthly, and monthly payrolls worth more than $6 million per month.

- Assist and advise clients with Human Resources issues, including paying terminated employees, new hire paperwork (W-4, A-4, I-9, etc.), name changes and name formatting for the Social Security Administration (SSA), and helping identify illegal workers through the SSA.
- Write letters to federal and state government agencies (IRS, Department of Revenue, etc.) responding to penalty notices or federal identification problems. Coworkers often reference past letters for helping write new letters.

(continued)

Submitted by Gail Frank

(continued)

JULI STOLSON, PAGE 2

- Provide virtually error-free work; results are dramatically less than the company's minimum allowed number of free services to clients due to processing mistakes.
- Selected and trained to be backup "Taxpay Specialist" as an extra responsibility.
- Chosen as "Garnishment Specialist" due to high level of accuracy and understanding of wage garnishment procedures.
- Developed organizational spreadsheet that kept track of amended clients' complicated previous quarter tax returns. It was adopted as the office standard.
- Earned 15 commendations from regional manager for excellent service above 90% as reported by clients on survey cards.
- Expedited a request, reprinted data, and hand-delivered a client's lost quarterly tax return package.
- Secured a 35% corporate discount for a client who confided business and financial troubles. Evaluated services client was using and recommended cuts for unnecessary charges.
- Completed pre-hire math test with a perfect score, when more than 90% of applicants fail the test.
- Passed year-long intensive training program ranked in the Forbes Top 100 Training Programs.

CUSTOMER CARE REPRESENTATIVE
I-PAY CHECK SERVICES
SCOTTSDALE, AZ (2000–2002)

Provided customer service for this check warranty company that approved checks for merchants like Best Buy and Sears. Resolved customer issues for angry and upset customers who had just had checks declined at a merchant that used I-Pay.

- Answered over 90 customer calls per day and resolved issues within the allotted 3-minute period. Assisted clients with returned checks and helped ensure future check acceptance.
- Earned 5 "Special Recognition" certificates for exceeding department standards.
- Received several complimentary letters from appreciative customers.
- Helped other order-processing departments with their workload. Deciphered detailed spreadsheets and ran complicated computer programs for deadlines.
- Volunteered for overtime during busy season; often worked 12-hour+ shifts.

EDUCATION & CERTIFICATIONS

GLENDALE COMMUNITY COLLEGE, Glendale, AZ, currently taking courses to complete accounting degree
PASCO HIGH SCHOOL, Dade City, AZ, high school degree, 2000
- Graduated with honors.
- Awarded Merit scholarship, which covered 75% of college tuition.
- Won award for creative writing.

Candidate is working toward her degree

This resume is a combination between chronological and functional formats

ROBYN L. WRYGHT

3673 Bay View • Canton, Ohio 44705
234.229.6811

The headline notes her job targets

OFFICE MANAGER / ADMINISTRATIVE ASSISTANT

Accounting — Payroll — Clerical Organization — AP/AR — Customer Service — Research & Writing

Experienced Business Office Administrator, exceptionally loyal and organized. Dedicated professional with proven administrative credentials. Demonstrates strong interpersonal and communication skills.

Professional Qualifications

- Ability to *communicate* with all levels of management and colleagues.
- *Management expertise* in all areas of office administration.
- Experience in situations demanding extreme *confidentiality*.
- *Interacts professionally* with clients, salespeople, vendors, etc.
- *Executes* multiple tasks and *expedites* in an accurate, timely manner.
- Proficient in *prioritizing* projects and schedules with positive *decision-making skills*.
- Skilled at *organizing* and *coordinating* professional/personal calendars, and following up with appointments and schedules.
- *Computer skills* include Microsoft Word and Excel; Peachtree and other basic accounting applications; familiar with network environments and e-mail/Internet.

PROFESSIONAL EXPERIENCE

CHROMATECH; Canton, Ohio
Administrative Assistant • 2002 to current
Provide all routine office assistance and functions in numerous cross-functional roles for international manufacturer of dies and pigments. Support sales team with correspondence needs, customer inquiries, and marketing materials.

- Function in all areas of accounting, accounts payable/accounts receivable, credit checking, and collections.
- Handle ordering of office supplies and purchasing of warehouse equipment as needed.
- Provide information and assistance to customers needing order/delivery and pricing help.
- Manage diverse special projects, presentations, and assignments.

CHEMCENTRAL; Columbus, Ohio
Assistant Office Manager • 1992 to 2002
Member of administrative team supporting one of the company's largest branches for national distributor of solvents and chemicals. Headed busy office with multiple cross-functional supervision and administration responsibilities.

- Oversaw accounting department clerks and activities to ensure accuracy and efficiency, including accounts payable and receivable, financial statements (monthly—yearly—taxes), payroll (attendance and hours for union—hourly—salary labor), journal entries, billing, and expenses.
- Assisted sales team and staff with research activities.
- Handled interoffice inquiries and internal conflicts to mutual resolution.
- Gave input on telephone systems and remodeling.
- Member of Quality Control Committee; investigated issues, gave advice, and resolved issues.
- Traveled to branch offices across the U.S. on special assignments.

Education was omitted because of lack of college degree (if it's not noted, it's not a focal point)

— *Excellent references available on request* —

Submitted by Lorie Lebert

LISA J. CARTER

185 Spring Lane ♦ Plantsville, CT 06479-1018 ♦ 860-555-2222 ♦ lisajcarter@hotmail.com

The top third of Lisa's resume provides critical information about the hard and soft skills she offers a prospective employer

ADMINISTRATIVE PROFESSIONAL

PROFILE

Detail-oriented, accurate, and observant. Well-organized and proficient at multitasking. Excellent customer service aptitude. Outstanding interpersonal and communication skills. Quick learner who can rapidly retain information. Team player who easily establishes rapport and trust. Bilingual—English and Spanish. Computer skills include Microsoft Word, Excel, PowerPoint, and Outlook. Part-time student available for first and second shift.

CORE SKILLS

- Administrative Support
- Procedure Development
- Appointment Scheduling
- Correspondence
- Research & Analysis
- Event Coordination
- Customer Service
- Record Keeping
- Reception

EMPLOYMENT HISTORY

Employment history is presented in an easy-to-follow format

CONNECTICUT SAVINGS BANK   Hartford, CT   9/02 to Present
Administrative Assistant—Mortgage Department

- ❑ Process and prepare correspondence and documents for department director.
- ❑ Organize new client files. Maintain and update existing files and records.
- ❑ Respond to clients' in-person and phone inquires. Provide rate information.
- ❑ Conduct ongoing research on competitor products and services.
- ❑ Orchestrate administrative functions, including appointment scheduling, filing, and faxing.
- ❑ Arranged office promotional events, including Mortgage Education Night.
- ❑ ***Researched and wrote 27-page office procedure manual adopted for use by 10 branches.***

THE COFFEE STAND   Waterbury, CT   5/90 to 9/02
Shift Supervisor/Sales Associate

- ❑ Oversaw activities, efforts, and training of 12 sales associates.
- ❑ Coordinated assignments and work schedules. Addressed and corrected shift problems.
- ❑ Assisted with processing customer orders, cleaning, and stocking.
- ❑ Balanced cash registers and processed bank deposits.
- ❑ ***Received 2001 Employee of the Year Award in recognition of 55% sales increase.***

Achievements in both positions are quantified and emphasized in boldface italics

EDUCATION

SOUTHERN CONNECTICUT STATE UNIVERSITY, New Haven, CT
Completing Master of Science (Part Time) ♦ Anticipated Date of Graduation—May 2008 (GPA 3.9/4.0)

UNIVERSITY OF CONNECTICUT, Storrs, CT
May 2004 ~ **B.A. in History** (GPA 3.2/4.0)

Submitted by Ross Primack

CARLOS PEREZ *The contact information is offset so the person's name gets more notice*

805-384-6397 • carpe4@aol.com

CAREER PROFILE:

Experienced professional with 16 years of experience in accounting, including responsibility for organizational budget oversight, reporting procedures systems, financial statements and analysis, audits, and payrolls. Proficient in MS Access, MS Excel, Quicken, Outlook, Lotus Notes, Smart Stream, SQL, and DB2.

AREAS OF EXPERTISE: *"Areas of Expertise" heading maximizes the impact of the candidate's skills and expertise*

- ➢ P&L Management
- ➢ Budget Preparation / Administration
- ➢ Auditing and Compliance
- ➢ Reporting and Documentation
- ➢ Financial Management / Forecasting
- ➢ Business Valuations

EXPERIENCE:

Senior Accounting Manager
Amplex Corrugated Products, Inc., Manassas, VA (1997–Present)
Responsibilities include

Indented text makes the format easier to read
- ➢ Management of monthly and yearly review of accounts receivable and payable for $150M budget of midsize manufacturing company.
- ➢ Designed and implemented annual planning processes.
- ➢ Directed gathering and analysis of relevant financial data from seven departments to support annual planning process.
- ➢ Developed new accounts reporting system to streamline data-gathering and reporting, resulting in 20% increased efficiency.
- ➢ Implemented training for accounting staff in new MS Access software that reduced data-entry hours and errors.
- ➢ Supervised staff of 10, including hiring, training, and promoting.

Finance Manager
Springfield Garden Supply, Inc., Manassas, VA (1988–1997)
Responsibilities included
- ➢ Oversight of bank reconciliation, accounts payable, general ledger account review, and state and federal tax compliance.
- ➢ Designed general ledger procedure manual and provided staff training.
- ➢ Developed plan for comprehensive audit system while facilitating communication between internal and external auditors.
- ➢ Designed new system for year-end physical inventory, cutting time from 10 to 6 days.
- ➢ Recruited, trained, and supervised staff of six.

EDUCATION:

Virginia Polytechnic University, Fairfax, VA
Master of Science in Information Systems Management (1998)
Bachelor of Science in Accounting (1986)

REFERENCES: Available upon request

Submitted by Mary Hayward

Susan Danville

906 Riverview Road • San Ramon, CA 97786 • 974.588.9900
sdanville@cox.net

Professional Summary

Accounting/Finance Professional with expertise in general accounting, financial analysis and reporting, financial systems, budget preparation, and cash management. Currently pursuing MBA in finance. *— Current pursuit of*

- Well versed in accounting principles, practices, and systems, as well as business operations. *MBA is emphasized*
- Team player who performs at high levels of productivity in fast-paced environments without missing a single deadline.
- Effective communicator and relationship builder with management, customers, staff, and financial institutions.
- Recognized for leadership and problem-solving strengths, as well as thoroughness and accuracy.

Experience

THE LYDEN COMPANY, San Francisco, CA   1983–2006
Senior Accountant   1991–2000
Accountant   1987–1991
Accounting Technician

Promoted through progressively responsible positions in accounting department in recognition of consistent performance results. Accomplishments: *Bulleted areas under experience focus on accomplishments*

Accounting/Auditing

- Managed accounts payable disbursements totaling more than $1.7 million annually, accounts receivable processing, and over $1 million in capital assets.
- Verified and maintained GL system. Developed and implemented accounting policies/procedures.
- Instituted internal control procedures, including suspense account reconciliations for premium collections, reducing write-offs by $75,000 annually.
- Coordinated audits with internal/external auditors and regulatory agencies. Compiled financial data for auditors. Prepared internal audit reports.

Financial Analysis & Reporting

- Coordinated and prepared NAIC financial statements in accordance with SAP and premium tax return filings for more than $1.8 million in 48 states.
- Prepared financial statements in accordance with GAAP for the Board of Directors and shareholders and semiannual SEC filings for 6 portfolios totaling $1+ billion in net assets.
- Analyzed and prepared variance reports for all management levels throughout business unit.

Cash Management/Budgeting

- Performed cash management functions to meet investment objectives and prepared timely corporate cash-flow forecasts.
- Developed and implemented banking policies for accounting, premiums, commissions, and benefits.
- Coordinated $35 million budget-preparation process for all departments within business unit.

Education

To avoid repeating similar responsibilities, a skills-based format was used to group together the last three job titles with one recent employer

M.B.A. candidate in Finance • Anticipated May 2006
Stanford University • Berkeley, CA

B.S., Accounting
California State University • Sacramento, CA

Submitted by Louise Garver

Juan Rodriquez

1221 Plymouth Road, Apt. 1305 ▪ Pembroke ON   K0K 4S1
j_rodriquez45@mail.com ▪ Telephone: 613 555-1010

Resume highlights skills and experiences that were specifically mentioned in the job posting

Press Operator

Specialty: Snap-sets ▪ Letterheads ▪ Statements ▪ Cheques

- Skilled **Press Operator/Pressman** with 8 years of industry experience; capable of working in a fast-paced environment.
- Strong troubleshooting and mechanical aptitude: able to solve minor mechanical and electrical problems on equipment.
- Proficient in the use of a variety of printing machines:
  - ✓ 10-Colour Sand Velcron U.V. 22" & 28"
  - ✓ 5-colour 22" Diddie
  - ✓ 3-colour Sanden Variable
- Excellent people skills: good listener, express ideas clearly and concisely
- Respected by peers, supervisors, and customers for industry knowledge and experience.
- Self-taught operator who learned to use and troubleshoot printing machines.

Clean and simple format reflects the candidate's personality

EXPERIENCE

Pressman
DataForms Inc., Ottawa, ON   Aug 98–Present

Joined company during start-up phase; observed machinery set-up and taught self to use equipment.

- Assisted with the design and layout of plant.
- Built workbenches and mastered trade through trial and error and observation.
- Regularly meet customers' deadlines.
- Read and interpret work-order instructions to ensure job is completed to customer's specifications.
- Operate machines with a capacity to run at 1,200 ft. per minute.
- Perform troubleshooting and maintenance on equipment—oil, clean, and make minor repairs.
- Constantly monitor machines to catch and correct production problems before they escalate.
- Examine samples to confirm that shades, colours, and brightness match customers' requirements.

EDUCATION & TRAINING

- **Pembroke Pines Secondary School** (1997)
- Specialized in Graphic Design & Printing

Submitted by Daisy Wright

Dan T. Harper

265 Charlotte Street, Asheville, NC 28801
(828) 254-7893 *Home,* (828) 230-1421 *Cell*

Heavy Equipment Operator

"I could pick an egg up off the ground and not break it."

Quote from the candidate himself speaks to his high skill level

PROFILE

DEPENDABLE, PATIENT HARD-WORKER with 32 years of experience in aggregate business operating **Drag Line** (9 years), **988 Loader** (7 years), **Hydraulic Shovel** (5 years), **Crane** (3 years), **Bulldozer** (3 years), **Trackhoe** (3 years), **Off-Road Truck** (2 years), and **Jaw Crusher** (1 year). Experience on computerized equipment.

SUMMARY OF STRENGTHS

Summary shows exactly how he contributes to company profits

- At work 30 minutes early *always.*
- Willing to stay as long as it takes to get the job done.
- *Never* miss work.
- Willing to do whatever I'm asked.
- Machine-friendly—easy on equipment; keep it well maintained and clean. Often put on older equipment because I don't tear it up.
- Excellent record for safety of life and equipment.
- Friendly and even-tempered; get along very well with co-workers.
- Keep production as high as possible.
- Know the relationship to company bottom line.

WORK HISTORY

Loyal and loved by his company, Dan has worked for the same company his entire career

BOONE GRAVEL—Asheville, NC   1975–Present
Portable plant, a subsidiary of RA Julius Industries, Mooreville, NC

- Use crane to tear down rock crusher, conveyor belts, bends, loaders, and backhoes; transport plant to where it is needed and put it back up, as often as three times a year.
- Have worked on large and small projects all over North Carolina in all kinds of weather, including 7 degrees below zero.
- Projects include road and interstate highway construction (including pulling river stone out of rivers, crushing, and transporting to highway site), opening up new quarries (clearing land, removing overburden), and commercial construction.
- Train operators on trackhoe, loader, and off-road truck on safety and operation.

EDUCATION

ADDITIONAL TRAINING

City High School, Owensville, NC
High School Diploma**,** 1975

Hundreds of hours of training: North Carolina Safety courses (1-day annual refresher training).

Submitted by Dayna Feist

KEN SANBORN

97 Moose Trail Path ▪ P.O. Box 1020 ▪ Soldotna, AK 99660
H: (907) 260-5987 ▪ C: (907) 631-2701 ▪ sanbornhunts@msn.com

PROFILE — *Profile section clearly notes which jobs he is interested in*

Industrious and dependable professional with 2 years of oil field experience seeking position as a Driver, Technician, Roustabout, or Expediter. Safety conscious with a QHSE passport. Accustomed to working long hours with demanding schedules in harsh climates, and under challenging physical and mental conditions. Solid employment references, strong work ethic, and levelheaded. **Qualifications include**

- ► Valid Class A CDL with HazMat, Tanker, Combo, and Air Brake endorsements and have a perfect driving record. Current N.S.T.C., Hazwoper and H2S.
- ► 100% drug free, on random drug testing with Worksafe through the U.S. Coast Guard.
- ► No safety incidents during 2 years on the slope; traveled by helicopter daily in one work hitch.
- ► Certified in first aid and CPR with valid endorsements.
- ► Hold a 100 Ton Masters License from the U.S. Coast Guard and can operate other heavy equipment, including bulldozers, loaders, and backhoes.
- ► Knowledgeable about welding and can quickly learn new technical/mechanical skills.

HIGHLIGHTS OF WORK EXPERIENCE

Highlights demonstrate his endurance, physical strength, and ability to work under extreme conditions in harsh climates

- Completed 12-week hitches on the slope as both a Straw Boss and Helper in the past 2 years.
- Run a halibut charter service during the summers, logging 12–16 hours a day, 7 days a week.
- Currently serve as a Bear Guard and Wildlife Specialist and as a Big Game Guide.
- Raised and worked on family cattle ranch, performing tasks requiring physical strength and stamina.

EMPLOYMENT HISTORY

MOUNTAIN CAT ENTERPRISES, Helena, MN **Bear Guard and Wildlife Specialist**	2005 to Present
SCHLUTZ OILFIELD SERVICES, Fairbanks, AK **Straw Boss**	2005
ENERGY SERVICES CONTRACTORS, Anchorage, AK **Straw Boss and Helper**	2004
DEEP WATER FISHING, Seward, AK **Charter Operator**	1999 to Present
GREATER SOLDOTNA ALASKAN GUIDE SERVICES, Inc., Soldotna, AK **Big Game Guide**	1997 to Present
HALIBUT RUN CHARTERS, Juneau, AK **Deckhand**	1998
BIG BLUE WATERS CHARTERS, Ninilchik, AK **Deckhand**	1997
D-R-J RANCH, La Paz, CA **Ranch Hand**	1992 to 1997

REFERENCES AVAILABLE UPON REQUEST

Because of his diverse work history, often with short-term jobs, a functional format worked best for this candidate

Submitted by Jill Grindle

The Professional Profile captures some of her interpersonal/transferable skills

Susan R. Richards

6344 West View Road
Williamsport, MD 21795
(301) 555-5763

Professional Profile

Production and **assembly worker** with more than 20 years of manufacturing and pharmaceutical laboratory experience. Work independently in assembling detailed circuit boards and sensors while remaining focused on quality and productivity. Experience working with chemicals to mix materials and reagents. Able to meet tight production deadlines by anticipating needs. Maintain good working relationships with co-workers and managers. Possess basic computer skills.

Assembly Experience

Breaks out two possible career paths (assembly and laboratory) into separate functional sections

Senior Assembler, Mole Productions, Martinsburg, WV   1996–2006
- Built, tested, potted, and finished sensors for flow meters used by domestic and international waste and clean water treatment facilities.

Mechanical Assembler, Smith Electronics, Inwood, WV   1973–1986
- Assembled printed circuit boards for communications equipment.

Skills Set

- Used a variety of hand tools and equipment, including drills, sanders, Dremels, band saws, lathes, soldering guns, wiring cutting, and hot stamp machines.
- Mixed chemicals and poured molds for polyurethane and ceramic sensors, following written specifications.
- Followed blueprints and parts list to ensure correct assembly.
- Consistently adhered to procedures and guidelines established by ISO 9000 and Lean Manufacturing principles.

Laboratory Experience

Laboratory Technician, USDA, Kearneysville, WV   1995–1996
- Provided support and materials for research laboratories.

Senior Laboratory Assistant, Hardin Labs, Winchester, VA   1992–1995
- Worked as a member of the support group assisting with manufacturing vaccine.

Veteran's Hospital, Martinsburg, WV   1987–1992
- Worked on a government contract supporting various research laboratories.

Skill Sets

- Wrapped and sterilized glassware for laboratory use.
- Operated autoclaves, dryers, and washers.
- Mixed chemicals to make media and reagents.
- Cleaned and maintained work area to cGMP (current good manufacturing practices) and GLP (good laboratory practices) standards.

Education

Currently pursuing GED, Washington County Board of Education, Maryland

Submitted by Norine Dagliano

HERNANDO R. DIAZ

11 River Street, Apt. #3C
Chicopee, MA 01020

e-mail: hernandochef@verizon.net

Cell: (413) 229-4511
Home: (413) 227-1894

Career Focus: **CHEF de CUISINE**

Career Focus immediately indicates to the
employer the job level he aspires to

PROFILE

Profile provides highlights of his skills,
experience, and achievements that build
his candidacy for his job target

✓ Food services professional with over 9 years of progressive experience who enjoys experimenting with different flavors to create innovative dishes, with particular interest in Spanish, Italian, and Portuguese cuisines.

✓ Trained and worked for 2 years in positions of increasing responsibility at a restaurant rated as one of the "Top 50 Restaurants in the Pioneer Valley" by **The Valley Advocate.**

✓ Diligent and skilled at running a busy kitchen and staff while remaining calm under pressure at all times.

✓ Natural passion and flair for cooking; grew up helping to prepare ethnic family dishes blended with an ongoing interest in continuing to learn new culinary skills.

✓ Awarded a one-year scholarship to Holyoke Community College and won first place out of 14 high school teams with an authentic Spanish rice and braised beef dish in an *Entrees from Around the World Competition.*

PROFESSIONAL EXPERIENCE

RIVERA RESTAURANT, Springfield, MA
Sous Chef/Kitchen Manager

2001–Present

Took on increased responsibilities to become an instrumental member in running a small, family-owned restaurant. Organize and overlook kitchen tasks that include developing prep lists, assigning duties to staff, and ensuring appropriate inventory levels. Participate in creation of seasonal menus and provide feedback on success of newly introduced dishes.

- Created a Spanish fish dish with caramelized onions, roasted tomatoes, garlic, and potatoes in a red-wine sauce that became a popular menu addition. Developed other signature entrée dishes with authentic flavors.

- Helped to prepare desserts such as tiramisu, rum bread pudding, dark chocolate cake, and a pear-almond tart that won over a following of loyal customers.

NEVILLE BREAD COMPANY, Agawam, MA
Assistant Kitchen Manager/Bread Baker

1999–2001

Started out as an overnight baker, preparing breads and making pastries for wholesale and retail accounts. Ordered supplies and checked dry-goods stock. Later helped put together lunch menu with soups, salads, and sandwiches, and to-go suppers that included pasta dishes.

- Acted as resident expert on baking matters and taught others preparation methods.

JORGE'S ON THE GREEN RESTAURANT, Longmeadow, MA
Pantry Chef/Sauté Chef/Expediter

1997–1999

Landed a position as the youngest member of the kitchen staff for a regionally acclaimed restaurant featured in *The Springfield Republican, Greater Western Mass Fine Dining,* and *The Valley Advocate.* Performed basic kitchen tasks and later helped with food preparation. Learned how to make pasta from scratch and many fine arts of gourmet Italian cooking.

- Advanced rapidly in food handling and cooking responsibilities for demonstrating enthusiasm and natural ability to master complex food-preparation techniques.

High school experience is mentioned
because this shows a clear pattern
of his interest in
this field

EDUCATION & TRAINING

Coursework toward an Associate degree in Culinary Arts, expected completion by 2007

Certificate in Bread Baking & Pastry, 2000

Gained basic cooking knowledge from part-time jobs as Banquet Chef and Pantry Chef while in high school

Submitted by Jill Grindle

NOAH S. THOMAS

1029 Joshkate Avenue • Cincinnati, Ohio 45231
(513) 598-9100 • nst@printedpages.com

Profile

Customer-focused manager with diversified experience in the retail/grocery/convenience store and restaurant industries, including stores that sell gasoline. Excellent analytical and problem-solving skills. Dependable and self-reliant; work equally well independently or as part of a team. Quick to learn procedures and assimilate new product knowledge. Core competencies: operations, ordering and inventory control, merchandising, employee scheduling and supervision, payroll, and record keeping. Excellent communication and interpersonal skills; proven ability to teach, lead, and motivate others.

Experience

Job duties are kept in paragraph form while accomplishments are bulleted for emphasis

SUPERSPEED USA, Cincinnati, OH   11/03–Present
General Manager
Total P&L accountability for gas station/convenience store operation (open 24/7). Hired, trained, and supervised 15 employees.

- Reduced shrink 42% by implementing improved internal controls (inventory, receiving) and loss-prevention initiatives.

- Increased gross margin by more than 2% by focusing on fast-food area.

- Earned an award for highest increase in fountain beverage sales (out of 100+ stores in the district), 2 consecutive quarters.

FAST FOODS, INC., Cincinnati, OH   9/99–10/03
Unit Manager, Danny's Burgers
Directed the activities of 20 Customer Service Representatives and 2–3 Assistant Managers in all aspects of restaurant operations.

- Turned around a failing store through a combination of retraining, encouraging teamwork, and controlling costs. Offset losses, producing $7,300 profit the first month and consistent profits ranging from $2,900 to $10,000+ each month thereafter.

- Improved drive-through speed an average of 32%.

- Developed computer programs and spreadsheets to schedule employees and track sales by product category and vendor.

- Recognized as Manager of the Month several times.

Education

Lack of a college degree is downplayed

CLAREMONT COMMUNITY COLLEGE, Pigeon Forge, TN   1996–1999
Completed classes in data processing, accounting, marketing, and management.

Computer Skills

Proficient with MS Office (Word, Excel, Access), FoodSys, various Internet search engines, and e-mail programs.

REFERENCES AND ADDITIONAL INFORMATION FURNISHED UPON REQUEST

Submitted by Michelle Mastruserio Reitz

NATALIE P. COLEMAN

20 Second Avenue ~ Hoboken, New Jersey 08873 ~ 201-963-8362 ~ npcoleman@hotmail.com

SUMMARY OF QUALIFICATIONS

Motivated Customer Service Professional with several years of experience providing optimum levels of service to both internal and external customers. Resourceful and organized with excellent phone skills and a talent for resolving customer/client questions and complaints in a timely and courteous manner. Innovative, creative, intelligent, and disciplined with a proven record of turning disorganization and discontent into order and customer satisfaction. Developed an impressive record of advancement and achievement in diverse positions due to diligence, drive, strong work ethic, and creativity. Adept at quickly learning and applying new concepts, technologies, processes, and procedures. Highly skilled in dealing effectively with diverse clientele, including demanding clients with very discerning taste, business owners, city officials, and patrons of casual and fine-dining establishments. Technical proficiencies include MS Office, Photoshop, Illustrator, and Quark.

CAREER HIGHLIGHTS

The Career Highlights section takes information out of chronological order and places less emphasis on current position as a bartender

PLANNING ASSOCIATES
- ❖ Increased operational efficiency, communication, and employee morale by redesigning the entire work environment of one of the top ten Urban Planners in the country.
- ❖ Added value to the firm's end product and increased revenue by creating original watercolor portraits of employer's designs for presentation to clients.
- ❖ Ensured a seamless operation by recreating the firm's image library that was lost in a corporate relocation.

BISTROT LEPIC
- ❖ Promoted from Hostess to Manager of this top 10 fine-dining establishment within six months of employment.
- ❖ Saved over $13,000 in excess expenses as manager and increased clientele 50% after redesigning the interior to reflect a modern and aesthetically appealing atmosphere.
- ❖ Exceeded all expectations in this fast-paced, full-time position while balancing a full-time student course load.

THE DESIGN STUDIO
- ❖ Designed the Silver line of designer purses currently being sold in Saks Fifth Avenue, Bloomingdales, Neiman Marcus, and other high-end stores; designed the 12 purses in this line with an eye for detail and quality to suit the needs of discerning clientele.

THE PRINTING PRESS
- ❖ Promoted to Sales Representative as a result of ability to deal effectively with customers and provide suggestions to increase business.
- ❖ Worked with customers one-on-one to obtain their specifications and develop solutions that met their needs while remaining within their budget.
- ❖ Increased sales by translating marketing concepts into visually appealing materials; presented concepts via the use of various visual aids.

EMPLOYMENT EXPERIENCE

CHARLIE'S BAR AND GRILL, New York, New York   2005–Present
Bartender
- ❖ Currently managing the bar of this popular eating establishment working both independently and in a team capacity to serve up to 200 patrons and ensure customer satisfaction.

THE DESIGN STUDIO, New York, New York   2005
Purse Designer / Interior Decorator
- ❖ Provided exceptional levels of customer service for customers of this high-end design studio.
- ❖ Designed home interiors according to customer specifications, providing appealing design options that suited their specific needs and budget while working in the Interior Design branch.
- ❖ Created contemporary purses with rich fabrics and colors to suit the needs and taste of discerning clientele.

PLANNING ASSOCIATES, Hoboken, New Jersey   2002–2004
Corporate Consultant / Image Coordinator
- ❖ Served as the front-line point of contact for new and existing customers of this top ten urban planner; fielded a high volume of calls and requests from city officials ensuring a smooth and efficient operation and maintaining the firm's professional image.
- ❖ Used Photoshop, Illustrator, Quark, and PowerPoint to edit images for client presentations.

(continued)

Submitted by Erika Harrigan

(continued)

NATALIE P. COLEMAN

The Employment Experience section emphasizes her dealings with customers

BISTROT LEPIC, New York, New York   1998–2000
Manager
- ❖ Recruited as Hostess and promoted to Manager within six months of employment as a result of providing exceptional customer service.
- ❖ Learned all aspects of the business to ensure that the needs of both the kitchen and the customers were met and to ensure a pleasurable dining experience for all patrons.
- ❖ Ensured a seamless operation by supervising and scheduling a staff of 30 waiters and effectively managing employee conflicts.

THE PRINTING PRESS, Jersey City, New Jersey   1997–1998
Sales Representative / Design Coordinator
- ❖ Interacted heavily with customers over the phone to receive orders and resolve complaints for this full-service commercial printing company.
- ❖ Promoted to Sales Representative charged with working one-on-one with customers to obtain their specifications and develop solutions that met their needs while remaining within their budget.
- ❖ Used PhotoShop and Illustrator to design flyers, brochures, and other visually appealing marketing documents for customers.

FERRARI CONSTRUCTION INC., Elizabeth, New Jersey   1995–1998
Personal Assistant
- ❖ Played an integral role in ensuring the success of this highly successful single-family home-building and masonry company by managing the billing, payroll, spreadsheets, and several other administrative details.

EDUCATION

PARSON'S SCHOOL OF DESIGN, New York, New York, 1998–2001
Studied Painting, Art, Graphic Design, and Textiles
- ❖ Commissioned by the college to represent the Mixed Media department by designing a statue.
- ❖ Created a piece of Color Theory artwork that was purchased by Newark Airport.
- ❖ Designed a mural currently located in the lobby of the Hoboken City Council.

COMMUNITY SERVICE ACTIVITIES

- ❖ Demonstrated leadership skills by donating more than 600 hours of community service.
- ❖ Served as Vice President of Walktoberfest and participated in beach sweeps, the Special Olympics, and tutoring mentally challenged individuals.

Candidate wants to transition from technical support to hospitality

MICHAEL R. BARKER
1411 Washington Street, Unit 3
Boston, MA 02118

(781) 264-4474   mikebarker@hotmail.com

FOOD AND BEVERAGE SALES AND DISTRIBUTION

Creative professional with technical credentials and a degree in food and hospitality looking to transition back into the hospitality industry. Highly motivated and creative with excellent written and verbal communications capabilities and strong interpersonal relationship skills. An analytical thinker with problem-solving skills and the motivation to succeed. A team player able to perform with minimal direction.

Resume highlights transferable skills while deemphasizing specific technical capabilities

EDUCATION

BA, Hospitality Management—Johnson and Wales University, Providence, RI
AS, Hotel/Restaurant Management—Johnson and Wales University, Providence, RI
Microsoft NT—Sullivan and Cogliano, Waltham, MA
Microsoft Windows—Boston University, Boston, MA

Education is placed near the beginning to highlight formal training in hospitality

PROFESSIONAL EXPERIENCE

Fidelity Investments, Boston, MA   2003–Present
Software Support Analyst

Responsible for providing PC and network support for 1,300 clients in the corporate office.

- Collaborated with engineers and software development to support the installation and integration of new enterprise applications.
- Acquired knowledge required to grow into a team leader.
- Coordinated teams to continually assess needs, identify resources, create schedules, monitor progress, and ensure resolution/fulfillment.
- Managed conversion teams to assist in migrating to new hardware and software systems.

Fresenius Medical Care North America, Lexington, MA   2000–2003
Senior PC Support specialist

Supplied PC and network support for more than 600 users in the corporate office—including troubleshooting hardware and software issues—and provided additional support for dialysis clinics and warehouses throughout the country.

- Managed software license compliance and ensured hardware standardization to maintain quality control.
- Researched, evaluated, and recommended new technology and managed technology agreements with vendors.
- Collaborated in needs assessments for new operating systems; supported these programs to ensure the technology met staff efficiency goals and lowered operating costs.
- Performed routine ongoing analysis to ensure that planned and actual expenditures met approved goals for performance.
- Conducted training sessions to ensure the proper use of company systems.

(continued)

Submitted by Judit Price

(continued)

MICHAEL R. BARKER   **Page 2**

CB Square Publications, Middletown, NY   1999–2002
Field Representative
Responsible for account support and developing prospects for a firm that serves the
strategic communications and information technology needs of school districts, not-for-
profits, and small to medium business.
- Communicated with customers to advise on and resolve product-related issues.
- Updated and maintained company managed websites.

Harrison Conference Services, Bank Conference Center, Waltham, MA   1998–2000
Account Manager/Operations Director
Responsible for the day-to-day operations of the facility. Managed a staff of 10 employees.
- Planned, coordinated, and delivered a range of conference activities.
- Contacted and qualified vendors, negotiated contracts, and provided oversight for all
  vendor service agreements.
- Recruited, hired, and trained the staff; processed payroll and benefit documentation
  and produced weekly and monthly status reports for management review.
- Instituted employee incentive programs and encouraged formal meetings to identify
  and implement areas of improvement.

South Management Services, Harvard Law School, Cambridge, MA   1996–1998
Assistant Food and Beverage Director
Assisted in directing the food service operation. Responsibilities included personnel, office
administration, marketing and sales, purchasing, security, and maintenance of the NCR
system. Managed a staff of 35.
- Recruited, hired, and trained new employees.
- Managed all funds and processed all reports; designed software to track and monitor
  inventories to reduce waste, yet maintain adequate supplies.
- Developed an ongoing set of promotions and innovative programs that increased
  sales. "Theme days"—with special menus, décor, and music—were very well
  received by the patrons. Expanded liquor sales by 10–15%.
- Established a planning process to ensure available staff for off-peak high-volume
  occasions.

Sports Service, Fleet Center, Boston, MA   1995–1996
Assistant Food and Beverage Director, Luxury Suites
Supported all operational activities for the luxury suites. Managed a staff of 50.
- Directed all staffing schedules for the Bruins, Celtics, concerts, and other events.
- Organized all hot/cold food and beverage delivery schedules to ensure quality service.
- Managed all inventory, ordering, and receiving; monitored all beverages.
- Collaborated closely with the executive chef and the F&B director on cost control and
  food quality to ensure customer satisfaction.

This candidate successfully transitioned from janitor to medical assistant

SHAWNTA NICOLE MARION

789 Angel Lane   St. Petersburg, Florida 33733   (727) 555-1212   snm@yahoo.com

PROFESSIONAL OBJECTIVE

Seeking a position as a *Medical Assistant* for a Family or Geriatric medical practice that values compassion, dedication, integrity, and results.

EDUCATION

ST. PETERSBURG UNIVERSITY, ST. PETERSBURG, FLORIDA (2006)
DIPLOMA—Medical Assisting
❖ **EXTERNSHIP, Palms Cardiology Practice, St. Petersburg, Florida** —————
❖ Successfully attended college and never missed a day of class or externship.

She was hired full-time before even starting her externship!

COURSE HIGHLIGHTS

Anatomy & Physiology   Clinical Procedures   Medical Office Procedures
Practical Procedures   Health Care Automation

NORTH EAST HIGH SCHOOL, ST. PETERSBURG, FLORIDA (1996)
DIPLOMA—General Studies
❖ Successfully attended high school and never missed a day of class.
❖ Worked **25** hours per week and sometimes up to **40** while attending high school full-time, by doing cleaning duties at Lakewood High School in St. Petersburg.
❖ Earned *As* and *Bs* while in high school.
❖ Volunteered with geriatric patients in the nursing department at *St. Anthony's Hospital* in St. Petersburg.
❖ Provided services to patients such as helping them by ensuring their comfort and well-being, checking on them daily, and bringing them beverages.
❖ Praised by management and patients for my communication, caring, compassion, and self-management skills.

EMPLOYMENT EXPERIENCE

PINELLAS COUNTY SCHOOL SYSTEM, LAKEWOOD HIGH SCHOOL, ST. PETERSBURG, FLORIDA
Plant Operator (1996 to Present)
❖ Have never called in sick or missed one day of employment in TEN YEARS.
❖ Thoroughly cleaned 15 classrooms of 32 seats daily from 5:30pm until 10:30pm Monday through Friday.
❖ Used vacuum cleaners, mops, brooms, dust pans, and cleaning supplies to prepare the rooms for the next day's use.
❖ Utilized self-management skills to work independently every day.
❖ Consistently demonstrated personal pride, initiative, and drive to clean the classrooms to the best of my ability daily.
❖ Praised by two supervisors for my work ethic, dependability, and the quality control that I exhibit every day on the job.

Points out her stellar work ethic

COMPUTER SKILLS

Microsoft Office (Excel & Word)
Windows XP
Microsoft Outlook   Internet Research
Proprietary Medical Practice Management Software

REFERENCES AVAILABLE UPON REQUEST

Submitted by Sharon McCormick

After many years as a production engineer, Stan wanted to switch to IT

Stanley K. Larringer
176 Woodhaven Drive, Eatontown, NJ 07724
(732) 927-5555 • StanLarringer@bol.com

Web Applications Management
E-Commerce • B2B • Project Management

KEY QUALIFICATIONS

✓ **Technical Strengths:** Up-to-date, diverse training in e-Business Management coupled with years of experience in analytical, technical process engineering profession.

✓ **Project Coordination and Teamwork**: Highly productive in team environments as both team member and team leader. Efficient in handling multiple project priorities.

✓ **Communication:** Able to communicate technical information in an easily understandable way. Recognized for relationship building with team members and clients. An effective listener.

✓ **Personal Attributes:** Innovative problem solver. Committed to goal achievement. Dependable.

EDUCATION

His Education section shows that he has the technical training to segue into Web applications

☑ Cybersoft Internet Professional—CIP 1, Cybersoft, Inc., Woodbridge, NJ
Certified e-Business Architect, e-Business for Managers—December 2005
Certified Cybersoft Communications 1000—December 2003
Courses: Networking, Database, Web Development, Web Design, Multimedia, Internet Business

☑ Bachelor of Science, Industrial Engineering, Connecticut Institute of Technology

TECHNICAL SKILLS

e-Commerce: e-Business and B2B Infrastructures and Consumer Payment Protocols
Applications: ERP, e-Procurement, Selling Chain Management, Customer Relationship Management
Software Tools: MS Word, MS Excel, MS Access, HTML, FrontPage 2000, JavaScript
Operating Systems: Windows NT, Windows 2000, Windows 98

PROFESSIONAL EXPERIENCE

ENGINEERING SYSTEMS, INC., Astro Space Division, Eatontown, NJ   1988–2005
Manufacturing Engineer, Production Engineering Department

Provided assembly documentation and engineering floor support throughout all phases of production flow, including fabrication, assembly, and test operations, for manufacturer of diverse satellite products contracted by major government clients (USSA and U.S. Air Force).

ACCOMPLISHMENTS

- Promoted to Team Leader for new equipment installation and upgrades. Performed research and analysis, and tested in production mode. Full authority to sign off fully tested equipment.

- Reduced cycle time by 30% through development of assembly and test tolling. Improved recycle characteristics and cut hazardous emissions into atmosphere by 40%.

- Collaborated with 60-person design engineering team to ensure that designs were producible in manufacturing environment. Provided cost-effective manufacturing recommendations.

- Trained 8 entry-level engineers in 4-month period to prepare efficient, labor-effective work plans for multi-line production floor in 80,000-square-foot facility.

Accomplishments are given prime visibility in the Professional Experience section, showcasing the strengths mentioned in the Key Qualifications section

Submitted by Susan Guarneri

Table of keywords based on her volunteer work, research position, and previous teaching experience highlights words that closely relate to social work and counseling

SHARON PARKER

2807 Sky Park Manor
Houston, TX 77082
sharonparker@aol.com
Cellular: 713-758-4587

CAREER OBJECTIVE: COUNSELOR—Advocacy • Family Services • Children & Youth • Women

Client-focused young professional with degree in psychology, demonstrated leadership capabilities, and strong interpersonal communication skills qualified for entry-level position in individual, group, or family counseling. Displays high degree of professionalism and empathy when dealing with victims and general public; able to create positive and trusting environments. Sensitive to diverse cultural, ethnic, and social backgrounds.

Hands-on professional experience combined with academic training in the following areas:

- Referral Servicing
- Program Coordination
- Hotline Services
- Goal Planning
- Youth Development
- Public Speaking
- Data Collection
- Group Counseling
- Community Resources
- Crisis Intervention
- Research & Analysis
- Self-help/Empowerment
- Client Needs Assessment
- Advocacy & Linkage
- Client Coaching/Motivation
- Womens' Group Work

EDUCATION

Bachelor in Psychology with minor in Human Development & Family Studies
University of Houston, Houston, TX, 2006

Key Coursework: Introduction to Psychology, Social Psychology, Sociology, Abnormal Psychology, Personality Disorders & Physiological Psychology

PROFESSIONAL EXPERIENCE / VOLUNTEER WORK / ACADEMIC INTERNSHIPS

Volunteer, Houston Area Women's Center (HAWC), Houston, TX (2006)
- Aid female residents and call-in clients with crisis-intervention services. Conduct client needs assessment and provide one-on-one phone counseling on issues of domestic violence and sexual assault.
- Present callers and clients with service information, public education, and referrals to community resources and service providers.
- Extend additional support and assistance to other departments, including Childcare Advocate and Group Counseling.

Research Assistant, University of Houston, Houston, TX (2006)
- Part of research team collecting data and categorizing information for in-depth study of couples and their relationships. Study is being sponsored by American Psychological Association (APA) and will be available for national review.

Sales Lead Assistant, Worktree.com, LLC, Houston, TX (2001 to 2005)
- Provided daily database management, sales assistance, and client-relations support for fast-paced recruitment agency serving more than 13,000 members.

Teacher's Aide (Internship), Human Development Laboratory School, Houston, TX (Summer 2003)
- Helped lead teacher with daily activities, instructional materials, curriculum development, and general classroom activities for 15 to 20 elementary students. Attended skill development and Parent Advisory Board meetings.

Administrative Assistant, AG Edwards, Houston, TX (2000 to 2001)
- Coordinated seminars, lecturers, and informational events for existing and potential clients. Scheduled meeting and client appointments for investment strategy/portfolio evaluation sessions with prospective clients.

Held additional positions in retail sales and office administration to finance college education.

Creates assumptions about her personal strengths, such as focused, committed, hardworking, and driven

MEMBERSHIPS / AFFLIATIONS

Artistic & Marketing Director—Urban Students Association
Treasurer, Fellow Mentors, Inc.

Her leadership roles in student-based organizations show her well-rounded college experience and ability to take initiative

Submitted by Abby Locke

Resume language was chosen to strongly promote candidate's high scholarship, leadership, and related memberships to clearly emphasize his readiness to confidently pursue a successful career in law enforcement

Alfred David Burton

Current:
100 Harold Point Avenue
Warren, WA 00000
(444) 222–6666

alfreddburton@aol.com

Permanent:
222 Jonathan Drive
Midtown, OR 00000
(000) 000-0000

PERSONAL PROFILE

- ➢ Highly motivated to begin and achieve employment objectives in the criminal justice field.
- ➢ Proven experiences of working well under stressful conditions.
- ➢ Rule-oriented, fair, and disciplined in giving or carrying out orders.
- ➢ Dedicated, focused, and diligent in executing and maintaining the highest level of abilities to reach all planned objectives and goals.

EDUCATION

Stetson University, Warren, WA
Bachelor of Arts degree in **Administration of Justice**   May 2006
Horton-Davis College, Lafayette, OR
Major in **Criminal Justice** (Transferred to Stetson University)   2002–2003
LaBelle Prep Academy, Midtown, OR
College Preparatory Diploma   June 2001

Honors / Scholarships:

- • Stetson University, Dean's Scholarship, $6,000 per year
- • Horton Davis Scholarship, one year, $8,000
- • Horton Davis Grant, $1,000
- • LaBelle Prep Academy College Scholarship, $1,500
- • Grade-point Average: 3.8/4.0 (*magna cum laude*)
- • Dean's List, Horton Davis College and Stetson University, three semesters
- • Washington State Police Entrance Exam score: 90%
- • National and Oregon State Honor Societies
- • National Irish-American Honor Society

RELATED WORK EXPERIENCE

Department of Safety and Security, Stetson University, Warren, WA
Dispatcher   9/12/04–Present

- ▪ Dispatch vehicles to officers' campus beats and patrols.
- ▪ Capably relay emergency information to on-duty guards.
- ▪ Maintain day logs and incident reports.
- ▪ Keep professional radio contacts, serve as operator on emergency calls, and assist Warren Police with information on law violations.

Quote from counselor adds weight to his candidacy

"Alfred's integrity, sincerity, career focus, and personal achievements mark him for high success in life."
—Brent Keenan, Guidance Counselor, LaBelle Prep Academy

Submitted by Edward Turilli

| Alfred David Burton | (444) 222-6666 | Page 2 of 2 |

Washington Department of Environmental Management (D.E.M.), Warren, WA
Park Ranger, Lincoln Heights State Park—Level Three Supervisor   Summer 2005

- Confidently supervised and trained 12 new rangers, assigning patrols within 250-acre park.
- Accurately kept day logs, incident reports, and vehicle inspection sheets.
- Charged with first to respond, handle, and assist in medical emergencies and violations of law occurring in park while on duty.
- Served as eyewitness for Washington State Police and D.E.M. Enforcement.

Park Ranger, Lincoln Heights State Park—Level Two   Summer 2004

- Enforced and maintained park rules and regulations, reporting violations to a supervisor.
- Provided park rules of conduct and general information to 5,000 summer visitors.
- Monitored on-duty professional radio contact.
- Maintained and updated bicycle safety inspection sheets.

Svensen-Gustafson Investigative Services, Inc., Lafayette, OR
Security Guard   1/22/03–4/19/03

- Assisted Horton-Davis College Police with traffic control at large campus events.
- Ensured the safety of students and families during winter events and graduation.
- Patrolled designated college buildings for the well-being and safety of students and staff.

SKILLS

- Computer: MS Word, PowerPoint, Access, Excel, Internet search capability
- Experience with finance duties as ADJ club treasurer
- Excellent organizational and major project planning skills

ACTIVITIES / ACHIEVEMENTS

- Administration of Justice Club, Stetson University, Treasurer
- Student Ambassador, Stetson University
- Treasurer, Class of 2005, Horton-Davis College
- Student Ambassador, Horton-Davis College
- S.E.E.D.S. (Student Events Excluding Drinking Society) active committee member
- S.A.R. (Student Admissions Representative)
- Criminal Justice Book Club, Co-founder / President
- Division One Football Team, three years; Captain, senior year
- Division One Super Bowl Football Championship Award

> *"Rights that do not flow from duty well performed are not worth having."*
> —Gandhi

*Targeted keywords/phrases of young client's extensive criminal justice
experience raise him above average entry-level job candidates*

Clean, easy-to-read format—no frills, no fluff

TREVOR HANK WHITE

810 Lake Shore Drive, Evanston, IL 60612   713-555-1984   trevorbusiness@xlt.com

FOCUS   Management Trainee—International Finance
Finance Degree with Spanish Minor and International Business Certificate

QUALIFICATIONS

- Focused, disciplined, and competitive individual who is goal-driven and welcomes challenges.
- Outgoing, friendly, charismatic; strong relationship-building and interpersonal skills.
- Effective team leader and team member who strives for excellence in any endeavor.

EDUCATION

Northwestern University, Evanston, IL   **May 2006**
Bachelor of Business Administration
- Major: Finance   Minor: Spanish   Certificate: International Business
- International Study Program: Madrid and Barcelona, Spring 2006
- Major GPA: 3.77/4.0 Cumulative: 3.84/4.0
- Presidential Scholar Award for Academic Excellence
- Valedictorian Scholar for Academic Excellence
- Student Scholarship for Academic Excellence
- World Class Scholarship for Academic Excellence

Evanston Academy of Learning, Evanston, IL   **2002**
- State of Illinois Scholar; National Merit Scholarship Finalist
- Academic All-State Scholar; Advanced Placement Scholar; Spanish Language Scholar
- Valedictorian Award—4.34/4.0 (Weighted Grades)
- Baseball Athletic & Academic Achievement Award
- Academic All-State Baseball Team Captain
- Varsity Baseball—Team Co-Captain & Captain; played baseball since age 8
- First Degree Black Belt—Tae Kwon Do Martial Arts
- Classical Pianist at local and state competitions

CAMPUS ACTIVITIES

Northwestern University:
- Finance Committee Student Representative—Northwestern Alumni Foundation
- Sigma Alpha Beta—Active Member; Greek Week Coordinator; Committee Chair
- Greek Council Association—University Student Representative
- Dance Marathon—Personally raised more than $5,000 for Children's Hospital
- Northwestern Greek Council—Vice President of Operations

EMPLOYMENT

Candidate has a well-rounded background and is well suited for various types of management trainee/entry-level positions

Illinois High School Athletic Association, Springfield, IL, Summers 2003–Present
- Certified Baseball Umpire for high school baseball games in central Illinois.

Delta Gamma Alpha, Evanston, IL, 2004–2006
- House Hand in charge of preparing, serving, and meal clean-up for 120+ members.

Evanston Insulation Incorporated, Evanston, IL, Summers 2002–2005
- Laborer involved in tear-off, installation, and repair of commercial roofing systems.

Submitted by Billie Ruth Sucher

This college student is looking for an internship related to both her major and her minor

Angela L. Ferris

Permanent Address:
After May 2006
4190 E. Timberwood Drive
Grand Rapids, MI 49500   ferris@cedarville.com

Current Address:
Until May 2006
123 Main Street #3100
Cedarville, OH 45314

CURRENT FOCUS

INTERNSHIP: Four months of volunteer experience, serving people in need in an underdeveloped or developing country, preferably India. Have had a three-year calling to work with the poor and AIDS victims showing Christ's love by being His hands and feet. Eager to learn and serve in micro-financing.

SUMMARY OF ATTRIBUTES

- Passionate about serving the poor and AIDS victims in an underdeveloped country
- Able to achieve results independently and as a cooperative team member
- Caring
- Excellent time-management abilities
- Self-motivated & goal-driven to reach high achievement
- Good written, verbal, and interpersonal communications

EDUCATION

CEDARVILLE UNIVERSITY, Cedarville, Ohio
International Studies Major; Bible minor, Fall 2005 to present

GATEWAY COMMUNITY COLLEGE, New Haven, Connecticut
International Studies Major, Fall 2004 to May 2005

NORTHWESTERN MICHIGAN COLLEGE, Grand Rapids, Michigan
English classes, Fall 2003 to May 2004

GRAND RAPIDS CENTRAL HIGH SCHOOL, Grand Rapids, Michigan
Honor graduate, National Honor Society, Graduated May 2004

EMPLOYMENT HISTORY

- Piano Teacher, *FOOTE SCHOOL*, 9/04–4/05, New Haven, CT
- Cook & Cashier, *CEDARVILLE UNIVERSITY,* 9/05–5/06, Cedarville, OH
- Customer Service, *AMON ORCHARDS,* 5/05–8/05, Grand Rapids, MI
- Server, *BOB EVANS,* 3/03–9/03, Grand Rapids, MI

ACTIVITIES   *College activities related to her internship target are included*

- Trained with YOUTH WITH A MISSION (YWAM)—Axiom, a nonprofit Christian missions organization, for a year, including five weeks in South Africa, working with AIDS patients and orphans. This was an important time, giving and setting a vocational foundation for the future: loving Christ by helping those who cannot help themselves.
- CEDARVILLE UNIVERSITY—Involved in Women of Vision/World Vision, Photography Club, Campus Congress, Intercollegiate Council, traveling, reading, writing, film, guitar, discussions on poverty and development

EXCELLENT REFERENCES AVAILABLE

Submitted by Terri Ferrara

This resume for a college student seeking an internship showcases the fact that she is committed to her career and has the work ethic to back it up

School	Alexandra Tamburro	Home
Alexandra Tamburro '08		21 Sugarloaf Drive
19 Crossroads Drive	atamburro08@coastal.edu	Sugarloaf, NY 12906
Conway, SC 29526		Cell: 845.867.5309

Objective: Internship Opportunities

Eager to learn first-hand about government operations and gain insight into corporate culture and the international arena

PROFILE

Energetic and career-minded individual with an academic record that reflects responsibility, leadership, and active involvement in the school community. Offering disciplined work habits, a high level of initiative, and a demonstrated ability to balance competing demands. Background also demonstrates a consistent effort to contribute to activities that require sound judgment, resourcefulness, and a significant amount of coordination.

EDUCATION

Coastal Carolina University, Conway, SC   *(Anticipated Graduation)* **2008**
Candidate: B.S. in Political Science & Public Affairs *(Current GPA: 3.56)*
Minor: Spanish

Extracurricular / Leadership Activities	**Academic and Leadership Involvement**
+ Student Activities (Music & Interactive Chair)	+ Judicial Board Representative (elected position)
+ Student Activities Board Member	+ Study Abroad (six weeks in Peru)
+ Model United Nations Club, Public Relations Chair	+ Presidential Scholarship Recipient
+ Spanish Club / JV Softball	+ Prospective Student Overnight Host
+ Gold Key Society (candidate)	+ Orientation Leader
+ Big Events Volunteer Coordinator (2004/2005)	+ Resident Assistant (named RA-of-the-Month, 9/05)
+ Big Events Executive Board: Communications Chair	+ Relay for Life Entertainment Chair

Frankfort High School, Poughkeepsie, NY   **2004**
NYS Regents Diploma

Academic Honors & Affiliations	**Extracurricular Activities**
+ High Honor Roll / Honor Roll (2000–2004)	+ Freshman Senior Day Leader
+ Dean's List (2004)	+ Art Club / Retreat Leader
+ Spanish (three years)	+ JV Softball (3 years) / Captain (2003)

ADDITIONAL EXPERIENCE

Coastal Carolina Ambassadors—Sophomore Coordinator   **2004 to Present**
Represent the college at local high schools (Dutchess & Ulster County, NY) during college breaks. Deliver presentations to high school students, promoting academic offerings and discussing campus life. Responsible for contacting schools, coordinating visits, preparing summary reports, and meeting with head coordinator (senior-year representative). Position term continues through senior year and requires 10 hours of weekly work.

Students in Free Enterprise, *Coastal Carolina University*   **2004 to Present**
Team-oriented group that works on community-driven projects that promote free enterprise. Participate in regional and national SIFE competitions to present project results in front of numerous corporate executives. Current project (Edison Ethics) involves teaching high school students about business ethics.

Model United Nations Security Council High School Conference, *Conway, SC*   **Spring 2005**
Served as a high-school advisor/coach for this professionally run program that provides a realistic simulation of the UN's practices and procedures as well as the issues that it addresses. Worked with students to help them prepare for the conference by providing an understanding of the workings of the UN as well as the various implications of its actions. Gained experience as a Secretary-General, Parliamentarian, and Secretariat.

EMPLOYMENT

Herkimer Arts & Crafts, *Herkimer, NY (Holidays & Summers)*   **2002 to Present**
Coleman Staffing & Temp Service, *Mohawk, NY*   **Summer 2005**

VOLUNTEER

Socastee Elementary School, *Socastee, NY (Tutor/Arts & Crafts Leader)*   **10/05 to 5/06**
After-School Program: Worked with first, fourth, and fifth graders to help with homework and boost math and reading skills. Developed arts and crafts activities that were age-appropriate.

Submitted by Kristin Coleman

This resume for a graduating high school student demonstrates his strong skills and previous work experience

JOHN U. HIGHSCHOOL

(410)-666-7777
juschool@hotmail.com

333 Third Street
Baltimore, MD 21075

Retail Sales Clerk / Stockroom Helper

SUMMARY OF SKILLS

- Cashier experience
- Proficient in using computerized cash registers
- Accurate and careful in counting money
- Recorded daily cash activities
- Reliable, punctual, and steady worker

- Good customer service skills
- Honest and trustworthy
- Good attitude around customers, friendly and helpful
- Patient with ability to mediate stressful situations
- Courteous and confident

PROFESSIONAL HISTORY

McDonald's Restaurant, Baltimore, MD
2004–Present Cashier/Cleaner

- Greet customers and assist in order taking and menu translations.
- Provide excellent service in a high-quality, clean, friendly, and fun atmosphere.
- Prepare food and provide quality guest service.
- Recognized as Employee of the Month 2004, 2005.

Lifeguard, Baltimore, MD
Summer 2003

- Instructed children on rules and regulations of aquatic facility.
- Monitored pool area for violations and potential hazardous situations.
- Assisted in maintaining pool and recreation areas.
- Instructed summer swimming classes.

Child Care, Baltimore MD
Summer 2002

- Provided child care for several families after school, on weekends, and during school vacations.

EDUCATION/VOLUNTEER

- Skyline High School, Baltimore, MD, Graduation pending June 2006, GPA 3.0
- Big Brothers / Big Sisters
- Maryland Literacy Program

Submitted by Brenda Thompson

MARC SCHMIDT

8709 Bay Vista, Venice, Florida 34668
727-815-1307

MSchmidt@hotmail.com
Cell 727-243-5800

PROFILE

General Manager/CEO with more than 25 years of extensive experience in the automotive and recreational vehicle field. Confident, aggressive, and responsible leader who motivates others and is results-oriented.

Consistent track record of improving bottom line and profitability through hands-on management of employees, marketing, service, parts, and inventory for new and used wholesale and retail vehicle sales. Independent turnaround specialist who can do it all. Laser focus on financial statements and profit-and-loss results.

Seeking business owner who needs a GM/GSM/CEO to take full responsibility for success. Must have the authority to bring about changes needed to improve the service and delivery process, and be able to hold employees accountable.

Summary is written in a direct style and indicates that he prefers autonomy in his work

PROFESSIONAL EXPERIENCE

SALES MANAGER
LEISURE DAYS RV   2003–2006   Orlando, Florida

Challenge: Succeed at selling recreational vehicles despite no prior knowledge of the business and add industry knowledge of this booming industry to portfolio of skills.

Results:
- Year 1: Selected as "Rookie of the Year"; achieved 400% of goal.
- Year 2: Achieved "Top 20" status within company.
- Year 3: "Top 10"; ranked #2 YTD 2006 of 158 salespeople.
- Currently travel with the American Coach travel team and as a member of the Leisure Days exclusive Crown Club team.
- Ranked as the #2 Fleetwood and the #2 American Coach salesperson.

GENERAL MANAGER/PARTNER
VEHICLE MAX DEPOT   1999–2003   Orlando, Florida

Challenge: Build startup used-car dealership with partner as an interim business venture.

Results:
- Built business from scratch to profitable level.
- Negotiated licensing and location contracts, bought vehicles, and started up business.
- Managed budget, purchasing, sales, inventory, service, and parts.
- Hired, trained, and managed employees.

Resume uses a dramatic format of "Challenge" and "Result" because Marc is a problem-solver and has numbers and results to back him up

Submitted by Gail Frank

MARC SCHMIDT, PAGE 2

CEO/DEALER/GENERAL MANAGER
SCHMIDT CHEVROLET   1994–1999   Bentley, Georgia

Challenge: Increase dealership sales and profitability. Eventually secured financing and bought out dealership in 1996.

Results:
- Took dealership from $20K/month loss to $77K/month profit within 1 year.
- Hired, trained, and managed 40 employees.
- Handled all day-to-day operations, including service, parts, sales, inventory, accounting, body shop, and both new and used vehicle departments.
- Wrote, produced, and appeared in all TV advertising and managed all marketing efforts.
- Sold dealership in 1999 after significant area economic depression: 3 major manufacturing facilities closed and several natural disasters devastated the agricultural industry.

GENERAL MANAGER
ROGER COPELAND HYUNDAI   1992–1994   Houston, Texas

Challenge: Offered partnership and percentage of future profits to turn around this dealership that was losing money.

Results:
- Turned business around within 6 months. Changed from a loss of $125K/month to profitable venture.
- Hired, trained, and managed 45 employees.
- Created, wrote, and directed TV advertising and ran all marketing efforts.
- Ran all business operations, including inventory, P/L, hiring and firing, and factory communications.

GENERAL SALES MANAGER / SALES MANAGER / SALES REPRESENTATIVE
RAYMOND AMC/JEEP   1989–1992   Stuart, Florida

Challenge: Hired to help this struggling dealership that needed sales and service turned around.

Results:
- Increased sales from 8 sales a month to 33 sales per month.
- Hired, trained, and managed 8 employees.
- Promoted to Sales Manager and then to General Sales Manager. The owner functioned as General Manager, so there was no more upward mobility.

AVIONICS ELECTRICIAN AND PLANE CAPTAIN
UNITED STATES MARINE CORPS

Maintained aircraft and worked with pilots training for air-to-ground control for Marine and Navy personnel.

There are enough results that the employer will probably not notice that the "Education" section is omitted

Profile highlights his computer training and goals orientation, along with other desirable transferable skills

Mark W. Collington
1711 Crestview Road, Manhattan, KS 66506
785-532-5555 Home ▪ markcoll@popmail.com

Mark's challenge was in not finishing college and having minimal work experience

OBJECTIVE

Help Desk / Computer Support Technician position

PROFILE

- ☑ Recent computer center graduate with proven organization abilities.
- ☑ Demonstrated track record of achieving goals in a team environment.
- ☑ Highly motivated and dependable—able to take responsibility for projects.
- ☑ Proven skills in problem solving, team leading, and customer relations.

EDUCATION

Recent computer training (including coursework) is positioned for maximum exposure

Tri-State Computer Learning Center, Topeka, KS   2005–2006
Computer courses completed in
- ✓ Networking Essentials
- ✓ A+ Certification
- ✓ Intermediate Word 2003
- ✓ Beginning Word 2003
- ✓ Beginning Access 2003
- ✓ TCP/IP protocol
- ✓ Beginning Windows NT
- ✓ Administering Windows NT
- ✓ Windows NT Core Technologies
- ✓ Windows NT Support by Enterprise
- ✓ Beginning Business on the Internet
- ✓ Beginning FrontPage 2003

University of Kansas, Manhattan, KS   2003–2004
General first-year coursework in Bachelor's degree program.

EMPLOYMENT

A Cut Above, Topeka, KS   2005–2006
Receptionist/Cashier

- Successfully handled front desk and three incoming telephone lines for busy, upscale hair salon. Greeted and logged in steady stream of customers, coordinating appointments with hairdresser availability.

- Developed cooperative, team-oriented working relationships with owners and co-workers in this 8-station salon.

- Managed customer problems and complaints with tact and attention to prompt customer service.

- Experience gained in opening and closing procedures, cash register receipts, counter sales, light bookkeeping, and telephone follow-up.

Plains Soccer Camp, Manhattan, KS   2003, 2004 Summers
Trainer / Coach

- Assisted Women's Soccer Coach in 200-participant soccer camp. Worked with individuals as well as teams to improve their attitude and resulting soccer performance.

ACTIVITIES & AWARDS

Kansas Cowboys Soccer Semi-Pro Team—Center Half   2001–2005
- ✓ Team consistently ranked in top 10 semi-pro teams in the nation.

Manhattan High School Soccer Team   2000–2003
- ✓ Captain of team that won the state soccer title in 2001.
- ✓ Recognized as one of the top two midfielders in the state, 2002.

Submitted by Susan Guarneri

Candidate was leaving the navy and wanted to apply his skills in maintenance, materials, and operations management in the private sector

DAVID A. JONES

85 Ellington Street • Groton, CT 06098 • (203) 437-6779

MAINTENANCE / MATERIALS / OPERATIONS MANAGEMENT
Transportation ~ Shipping Industry

"David is an exceptional planner, organizer and innovative problem solver who has succeeded where others have failed ... he has exceptional operations expertise, strong leadership skills, and sound judgment."

—Bertrand Fisher
Commanding Officer

Management Professional offering 15 years of experience in electronics equipment maintenance, materials, operations, and security.

- Promoted through increasingly responsible technical and supervisory positions based on expertise, demonstrated initiative, and contributions to operational efficiency.
- Effective trainer who develops and leads staff to peak performance.
- Expert in navigation and ship-handling operations and systems.
- Recipient of 15 achievement, commendation, and distinguished service awards throughout naval career.

RELEVANT EXPERIENCE & ACCOMPLISHMENTS

Maintenance & Materials Management
- Improved operations through aggressive materials improvement and equipment refurbishment programs that were subsequently instituted throughout the organization.
- Supervised electronics technicians in maintenance/repair of various communications, radar, and other electronics systems, ensuring peak efficiency and reliability.
- Led implementation of efficient purchasing and JIT inventory management system.
- Oversaw hazardous cargo certification requirements, equipment maintenance, and safety deadlines.

Operations Management
- Managed the daily planning, coordination, and supervision of 45 staff members, effectively ensuring stringent compliance with vessel safety standards.
- Developed and executed detailed operational review plans for command administrative inspection, resulting in timely problem identification and corrective actions.
- Recognized for instrumental role in achieving "excellent" ratings in all areas during plant inspections.

Staff Training & Management
- Trained more than 500 military and civilian personnel in maintenance procedures, navigation, firefighting, damage control, security, and other areas.
- Turned around an underperforming division to rank #1 in productivity by improving the training curriculum.

CAREER HISTORY

United States Navy • 1989 to Present
Patrol Boat Captain • 1989 to 1990; Legal & Administrative Officer • 1988 to 1989
Assistant Operations & Electronics Material Officer • 1986 to 1988

EDUCATION

B.E., Electrical Engineering, Connecticut College • New London, CT
Additional Training: Electronics Material Management Training Program
Boat Group Management Training Program, Military Justice Legal Training Program

His actual job titles are listed under Career History to deemphasize them while translating his relevant experience and accomplishments into three skill sections to help the reader understand his background

Submitted by Louise Garver

This retiring army colonel had completed a successful command tour in Iraq and now was assigned to a staff leadership position in anticipation of his retirement

ARTHUR ANDERSON, JR.
2 Custer Avenue
Fort Riley, KS 66442
Home: 785-706-3100
e-mail: arthuranderson1@yahoo.com

OBJECTIVE

A management position in operations or logistics in the retail industry.

SUMMARY OF QUALIFICATIONS

Twenty-four years of experience in leadership, command, and senior staff positions in medium and large complex organizations. Versatile, dynamic leader and high achiever who communicated positively and effectively with people at all levels of an organization. Demonstrated record of success in creating highly effective teams, logistics management, strategic planning, increasing efficiency, and establishing strong organizational systems.

- **Logistics Distribution**
- **Leadership**
- **Strategic Planning**
- **Organizational Management**
- **Team Building**
- **Training**

ORGANIZATIONAL MANAGEMENT

Supervised all aspects of a large, complex organization of 6,000 personnel. Efficiently executed an annual budget of $42M. Implemented aggressive management controls and cost-reduction initiatives that resulted in the savings of an average of $1M per quarter. Maintained and operated facilities, complex equipment, and vehicles with a total value in excess of $500M. Planned, prepared, and executed organizational oversight for task forces and peace support rotations. Used an active and positive After Action Report process to ensure task forces knew what happened, why it happened, and how they could fix problems.

Writer chose to emphasize his skills in a functional format

TRAINING

Created an integrated team training approach to teach, coach, and mentor leaders of medium-sized organizations in all aspects of leadership and training. Prepared them to deploy to contingency locations to assist units as they complete preparations for war or peace. Created an environment where soldiers could focus on training to learn and gain confidence in their war-fighting skills while ensuring soldier and family readiness.

LEADERSHIP

Led and commanded small, medium, and large organizations of up to 6,000 personnel. Commanded a large multiservice organizational team of 6,000 personnel in Iraq and a medium organization of 1,000 in Bosnia. Coordinated the efforts and activities of army units, international humanitarian organizations, and nongovernmental agencies. Cited by General Officers for "always leading my soldiers from the front and never asking them to do anything I would not do myself" and "moving my command without regard for personal danger to ensure it was at the decisive point of the battle, at the right time."

Submitted by James Walker

ARTHUR ANDERSON, JR.

LOGISTICS DISTRIBUTION AND MANAGEMENT

Created and maintained a complex logistics distribution network with thousands of lines of supply both in the United States and Iraq. Aggressive leadership and planning ensured on-time delivery and minimal lag time. Implemented highly effective systematic maintenance procedures and user responsibilities in the supply warehouse, resulting in increased readiness rates and better asset visibility.

STRATEGIC PLANNING

Helped develop and execute the Fort Riley strategic training and logistics plans. Negotiated with numerous Iraqi, U.S. governmental officials, and other foreign nationals in planning and implementing a regional strategy for reconstruction. Responsible for administering $23.5 million in Iraqi reconstruction money. Effectively managed combat and civil affairs operations to support local governance initiatives as well as training for emerging Iraqi Security Forces.

TEAM BUILDING

Planned, funded, and constructed a series of bases in Iraq exceeding $20M. Teamed with the Corps of Engineers, international contractors, and organizational units to complete the projects efficiently and effectively. Fostered a sense of cooperation and trust with rotational units that fed on my infectious enthusiasm and passion for learning how to lead, fight, and win. Created a command climate that was professional, healthy, stimulating, and extremely supportive for young officers and junior leaders.

EMPLOYMENT HISTORY

- Director for Operations and Logistics, U.S. Army, Fort Riley, KS, November 2004–Present
- Commander, U.S. Army, Iraq and Fort Riley, KS, June 2003–October 2004
- Commander, U.S. Army, Fort Carson, CO, June 2002–May 2003
- Training Director, U.S. Army, Heidelberg, Germany, June 2000–June 2001
- Commander, U.S. Army, Bosnia and Fort Bragg, NC, May 1998–May 2000

EDUCATION

- Graduate, Military Strategic Studies, 1 year, U.S. Army War College, Carlisle, PA
- Master of Science, Strategy, U.S. Army War College, Carlisle Barracks, PA
- Master of Arts, History, Temple University, Philadelphia, PA
- Bachelor of Science, Engineering, United States Military Academy, West Point, NY

*Candidate's name and expertise stand out
in this bold presentation*

DOLORES SMITH

2092 Recreation Drive • Powell, Ohio 43065
Home: 614-890-4499 • Cell: 614-276-4544
e-mail: dolores@worthingtonma.com

COSMETIC ARTISTRY • COSMETIC SUPPLY SALES • PROFIT CENTER MANAGEMENT

Leading-Edge Cosmetology Techniques/Methods • Esthetics • Spa Profit Protocols

Customer-oriented cosmetology professional with valuable blend of business ownership and management experience combined with noticeable talent in esthetic skin care leading to enhanced appearance and well-being of customers; utilizing 25-year history as licensed **Cosmetologist, Manager, and Instructor** to propel all facets of client care, organizational management, and strategic planning agendas. Extremely well organized, dedicated, and resourceful with ability to guide operations and associates to **technique improvements, maximized productivity, and bottom-line increases.**

AREAS OF STRENGTH

- Relationship Building • Customer Service •
- Time Management • Creative/Strategic Selling •
- Follow-Up • Merchandising/Promotion •
- Relationship Management •
- Product Introduction • Inventory Management •
- Expense Control • Vendor Negotiations •
- Client Needs Analysis •

EDUCATION

FINER ACADEMY OF COSMETOLOGY ... Finer, Ohio
• Cosmetology • Manager • Instructor •
Licenses

FINER ACADEMY OF HAIR DESIGN ... Finer, Ohio
Graduate in Hair Design

SEMINARS & SPECIALIZED TRAINING

Continuing Education Units
(to meet requirements of 8 credits annually)

Certificate of Achievement for Advanced Basic
Esthetics and Spa Therapies, August 2004

Several seminars held by various cosmetics
associations

ADDITIONAL BACKGROUND

The Hair Artists ... Dublin, Ohio
Manager of Licensed Cosmetologists
(1993–1996)

Jean Benet Salon ... Worthington, Ohio
Licensed Cosmetologist
(1990–1993)

PROFESSIONAL EXPERIENCE

STUDIO D@RENÉ.....DUBLIN, Ohio (May 1996 to October 2004)
Full-service and independent customized hair, nails, and tanning boutique positioned in strip-mall (suburban locale) setting; operations staffed by 5 employees, contractors, and technicians.

Owner/General Manager
Directed total operation while simultaneously contributing as cosmetologist in one of four-station salon; as single owner of small business, administered profit and loss, undertook all facets of decision-making, strategically guided salon operations and productivity, and assumed complete responsibility for revenue performance.

Management responsibilities included cosmetic and accessories sales, customer service, client management, accounting, finance, recruiting/hiring/training/scheduling, compliance, business/operations legal requisites, retail merchandising, advertising, inventory procurement/control, vendor relationships, contract negotiations, booth rental contracts, and leases to licensed cosmetologists and nail technicians.

→ **Successfully conceived and launched full scale of operations** and guided business to strong reputation for quality output of product and services; consistently met challenges of market conditions and business atmosphere to persevere throughout 8 years of ownership.

→ **Maintained operating costs at lowest possible point by reducing inventory and labor hours during seasonal periods;** also negotiated with vendors to secure better pricing for goods and services.

→ **Facilitated revenue increase by bringing in cosmetic line to enhance product offering to clients.**

→ **Recognized revenue opportunity** and spearheaded remodel of existing tanning space to provide for salon.

→ **Expanded market visibility by becoming member of Powell Chamber of Commerce.**

→ **Modified policies and procedures to ensure employee compliance with changing licensing regulations.**

→ **Worked in concert with American Cancer Society to provide styling services to cancer patients** with aims at improving appearance, outlook, confidence, and self-esteem.

Two column-format enables her to pack lots of information on one page

Submitted by Jeremy Worthington

How to Contact the Professional Resume Writers Who Contributed to This Book

The following professional resume writers contributed resumes to this book. They are all members of the Career Masters Institute (www.cminstiute.com). I acknowledge with appreciation their well-written examples.

Tammy W. Chisholm, CPRW
MBA Resumes
P.O. Box 2403
Mechanicsville, VA 23116
Phone: (804) 878-9296
Fax: (320) 306-1752
E-mail: twchisholm@
mba-resumes.com
www.mba-resumes.com

Kristin Coleman
Coleman Career Services
Poughkeepsie, NY 12603
Phone: (845) 452-8274
E-mail:
Kristin@colemancareerservices.com

Denyse Cowling, CPC, RPR, CIS
Career Intelligence, Inc.
18-1275 Stephenson Dr.
Burlington, Ontario L7S 2M2
Canada
Phone: (905) 333-8283

Toll-free: (866) 909-0128
E-mail: dcowlings@cogeco.ca
www.careerintelligence.ca

Norine T. Dagliano, NCRW, CPRW, CFRW/CC
ekm Inspirations
14 N. Potomac St., Ste. 200A
Hagerstown, MD 21740
Phone: (301) 766-2032
Fax: (301) 745-5700
E-mail:
norine@ekminspirations.com
www.ekminspirations.com

Donna Farrise
President, Dynamic Resumes of
Long Island, Inc.
300 Motor Pkwy., Ste. 200
Hauppauge, NY 11788
Phone: (631) 951-4120
Toll-free: (800) 528-6796 or
(800) 951-5191

Fax: (631) 952-1817
E-mail:
donna@dynamicresumes.com
www.dynamicresumes.com

Dayna Feist, CPRW, CEIP, JCTC
Gatehouse Business Services
265 Charlotte St.
Asheville, NC 28801
Phone: (828) 254-7893
Fax: (828) 254-7894
E-mail: gatehous@aol.com
www.bestjobever.com

Terry Lynn Ferrara, CCMC
Your Career Coach
4190 E. Timberwood
Traverse City, MI 49686
Phone: (231) 938-0766
E-mail:
Terri@YourCareerCoach.com

**Gail Frank, NCRW, CPRW,
JCTC, CEIP, MA**
Frankly Speaking: Resumes That
Work!
10409 Greendale Dr.
Tampa, FL 33626
Phone: (813) 926-1353
Fax: (813) 926-1092
E-mail: gailfrank@post.harvard.edu
www.callfranklyspeaking.com

**Louise Garver, CPRW, MCDP,
CEIP, JCTC, CMP**
Career Directions, LLC
115 Elm St., Ste. 103
Enfield, CT 06083
Phone: (860) 623-9476
Fax: (860) 623-9473
E-mail: louisegarver@cox.net
www.careerdirectionsllc.com

**Wendy Gelberg, M.Ed., CPRW,
IJCTC**
President, Advantage Resumes
21 Hawthorn Ave.
Needham, MA 02492
Phone: (781) 444-0778
Fax: (781) 444-2778
E-mail: WGelberg@aol.com

Don Goodman, CPRW, CCMC
About Jobs
18 Eaton Dr., Ste. 201
N. Caldwell, NJ 07006
Toll-free: (800) 909-0109
Toll-free fax: (877) 572-0991
E-mail:
dgoodman@GotTheJob.com
www.GotTheJob.com

Jill Grindle, CPRW
Resume Inkstincts
Agawam, MA 01001
Phone (413) 789-6046
Fax: (203) 413-4376
E-mail:
j.grindle@resumeinkstincts.com
www.resumeinkstincts.com

**Susan Guarneri, NCCC,
NCC, DCC, CPRW, CERW,
CPBS, CCMC**
Guarneri Associates
6670 Crystal Lake Rd.
Three Lakes, WI 54562
Toll-free: (866) 881-4055
Fax: (715) 546-8039
E-mail: susan@resume-magic.com
www.resume-magic.com

Erika C. Harrigan, CPRW
Success Partners
P.O. Box 212
Franklin Park, NJ 08823

Phone: (732) 501-0375
Fax: (732) 783-0229
E-mail: eharrigan@
successpartnerservices.com
www.successpartnerservices.com

Mary E. Hayward, CPRW, JCTC, CMBTI
Career Options
18 Canoe Brook Rd., Apt. 17
Putney, VT 05346
Phone: (802) 387-3396
Fax: (802) 258-3252
E-mail: mary.hayward@sit.edu
www.gethiredresumes.com

Gay Anne Himebaugh
Seaview Résumé Solutions
2855 E. Coast Hwy., Ste. 102
Corona del Mar, CA 92625
Phone: (949) 673-2400
Fax: (949) 673-2428
E-mail: resumes@
seaviewsecretarial.com
www.scaviewsccrctarialsolutions.
com

Lorie Lebert, CPRW, IJCTC, CCMC
THE LORIEL GROUP
P.O. Box 91
Brighton, MI 48116
Phone: (810) 229-6811
Toll-free: (800) 870-9059
E-mail: Lorie@ResumeROI.com
www.CoachingROI.com

Abigail Locke, CARW, CFRW
Premier Writing Solutions, LLC
Phone: (202) 635-2197
Toll-free fax: (866) 350-4220
E-mail: info@premierwriting.com
www.premierwriting.com

Sharon McCormick, MCC, NCC, NCCC, CPRW
Sharon McCormick Career and
Vocational Consulting Services
1061 85th Terrace N. #D
St. Petersburg, FL 33702
E-mail: career1@ij.net

Don Orlando, MBA, CPRW, JCTC, CCM, CCMC
The McLean Group
640 S. McDonough St.
Montgomery, AL 36104
Phone: (334) 264-2020
Fax: (334) 264-9227
E-mail: yourcareercoach@
charterinternet.com

Judit E. Price, MS, IJCTC, CDFI, Personal Branding Specialist
Berke & Price Associates
6 Newtown Way
Chelmsford, MA 01824
Phone: (978) 256-0482
Fax: (978) 250-0787
E-mail: jprice@careercampaign.com
www.careercampaign.com

Ross Primack, CPRW, CEIP, GCDF
Connecticut Dept. of Labor
200 Folly Brook Blvd.
Wethersfield, CT 06109-1114
Phone: (860) 263-6041
E-mail: ross.primack@ct.gov
www.ctdol.state.ct.us

Laura Smith-Proulx, CPRW
Evans Resumes/Career Change
Resumes
15400 W. 64th Ave., Ste. E9 #164
Arvada, CO 80007
Toll-free: (877) 258-3517

Toll-free fax: (866) 374-4428
E-mail: info@evansresumes.com
www.evansresumes.com

Michelle Mastruserio Reitz, CPRW
Printed Pages
3985 Race Rd., Ste. 6
Cincinnati, OH 45211
Phone: (513) 598-9100
Fax: (513) 598-9220
E-mail: michelle@printedpages.com
www.printedpages.com

Billie Ruth Sucher, MS, CTMS, CTSB, JCTC
Billie Ruth Sucher & Associates
7177 Hickman Rd., Ste. 10
Urbandale, IA 50322
Phone: (515) 276-0061
Fax: (515) 334-8076
E-mail: billie@billiesucher.com

Brenda Thompson, MS, CCMC
TH and Associates
P.O. Box 1043
Bowie, MD 20718
Phone: (301) 266-1115
Fax: (301) 352-6135
E-mail: thworks@comcast.net
www.thworks.net

Edward Turilli, MA
Director Career Development
Center, Salve Regina University
100 Ochre Point Ave.
Newport, RI 02840
Phone: (401) 341-2203
E-mail: edtur@cox.net
www.resumes4-u.com and
www.careers4-u.com

James Walker, MS
Counselor, ACAP Center
Bldg. 210, Rm. 006, Custer Ave.
Ft. Riley, KS 66442
Phone: (785) 239-2278
Fax: (785) 239-2251
E-mail: jwalker8199@yahoo.com

Jeremy Worthington
Buckeye Resumes
2092 Atterbury Ave.
Columbus, OH 43229
Phone: (614) 861-6606
Fax (614) 737-6166
E-mail:
Jeremy@buckeyeresumes.com

Daisy Wright, CDP
The Wright Career Solution
Brampton, ON, L6Z 4V6
Canada
Phone: (905) 840-7039
E-mail:
careercoach@thewrightcareer.com
www.thewrightcareer.com

Index

© JIST Works